Computer Repair with Diagnostic Flowcharts – Revised Edition

Troubleshooting PC Hardware Problems from Boot Failure to Poor Performance

Morris Rosenthal

Please Read

The author has done his best to provide accurate and up-to-date information in this book, but he cannot guarantee that the information is correct or will fit your particular situation. The book is sold with the understanding that the publisher and the author are not engaged in rendering professional or engineering services. If expert assistance is required, the services of a competent professional should be sought.

Flowcharts produced with Microsoft Visio Standard

Published by Foner Books

www.fonerbooks.com

ISBN 0-9723801-7-5

Instructions

This book was not designed to be read from cover to cover. At the core of the book are seventeen diagnostic flowcharts, and the sole purpose of the text is to expand upon them. The flowcharts themselves are necessarily written in short-hand form, to fit a meaningful number of decision points on a page. A linear text is simply not possible due to the decision tree structure of the flowcharts. The diamond shape for each decision point in the flowchart is repeated in the outer margin of the following pages. This marks the section of text that explains the action in more detail. Do not read beyond the designated section without returning to the flowchart to determine the next step.

The ovals in the flowcharts contain instructions or suggestions. If a suggestion like "reseat the cable" doesn't work, the best course is to return to the previous decision point and continue with the diagnostic down the other branch. These charts are designed to push parts swapping to the end of the diagnostic procedures wherever possible, so readers without a stock of spare parts will have the best chance to repair the problem without spending money. You should always label any parts you remove from a machine as "suspicious," and if it becomes apparent that they are truly faulty, dispose of them.

The "home plate" symbol is used in flowcharts to transfer control to an off-chart point. Most of the flowcharts in this book have multiple decision paths that will send you to a different flowchart for a different hardware sub-system. As with the suggestion oval, if you've already been there, you can retreat to the last decision point and determine if following the other branch makes sense.

Diagnosis is an art. There's no point in having the world's leading brain surgeon poking around in your skull if the problem is with your liver. This is exactly analogous to what happens when techs or hobbyists troubleshoot PCs without following some intelligent diagnostic procedure. The most experienced techs are sometimes some of the worst diagnosticians, because they're overconfident in their troubleshooting abilities. If you work on a given brand of PCs for a few months and you find that 90% of the problems encountered are due to a bad power supply, you start attributing all PC problems to power supplies. If you'd been working in a different shop on a different brand, you may have concluded that 90% of all computer problems were due to bad RAM, etc. You should always approach each new problem with an open mind and look at the most basic possibilities before jumping to conclusions.

This book focuses on ATX PCs with a modern plug-n-play motherboard and BIOS. These PCs first appeared in the mid-90's and still accounted for all of the standard PCs sold in 2008. ATX computers are turned off and on by a switch on the front panel of the PC which tells the motherboard to instruct the power supply to come full on. An ATX power supply is always supplying a trickle of current to the motherboard as long as it's plugged in and the override switch on the back of the supply isn't turned off. To avoid the risk of damaging components when working in the PC, unplug the power supply before making any changes inside the case.

Since unplugging the PC removes the ground, this increases the risk of damaging components with a static electric discharge. In over 20 years of working on PCs I've only zapped one component that I know of, a SCSI hard drive, and that was in a high static environment. Don't work in a dry area with a rug or rub Styrofoam all over your body before picking up a part. Don't work in an area where you frequently experience static electric shocks. It's good to form the habit of touching some exposed piece of metal, even if it's not grounded itself, before picking up static sensitive devices. If you don't have much experience working around computer parts and the static threat worries you, buy a static bracelet and tether at the local electronics store for a few dollars.

You need to have a basic knowledge of the terminology of computers and the physical appearance of PC components to benefit from these flowcharts. This book is not for beginners, but we have added links to illustrated procedures on the publisher's website, fonerbooks.com. Many of the procedures described in this book require a basic knowledge of working with electronics. Procedures describing live power and bench testing may result in harm to the computer hardware, the tester (you), and the environment (your house).

The vast majority of ATX PCs run some version of Microsoft Windows. Therefore, when it's necessary to refer to the operating system, the references are usually to Device Manager, the standard Windows hardware manager through Windows Vista and likely beyond.

Power Supply Failure

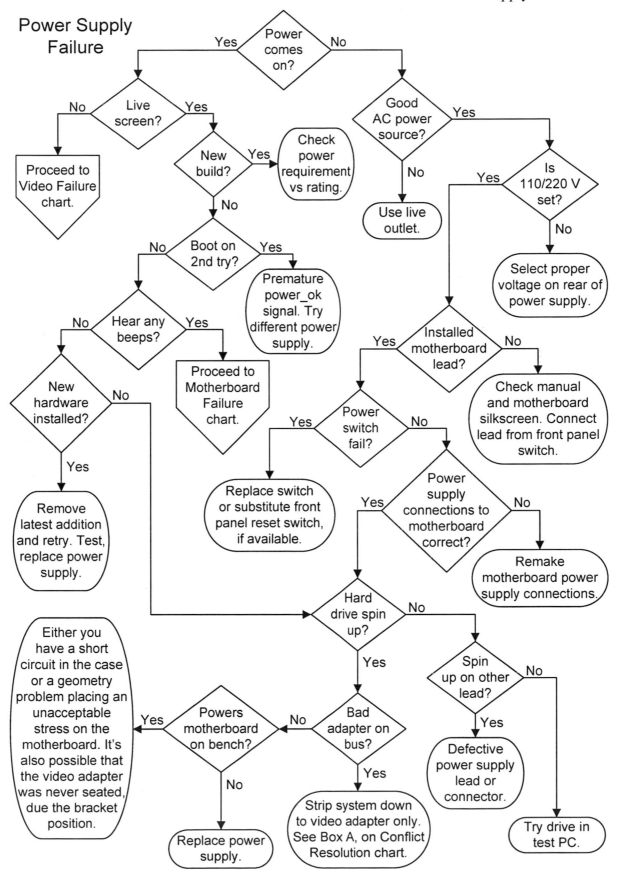

Power Supply Failure

The first step in power supply diagnostics is determining whether or not the power comes on. How can you tell if the power is on? Can you hear fans turning and drives motors spinning up, see little lights on the front of the CPU case or hear any beeps? If the system case is hot (if you get a shock) pull the plug immediately - you have a ground failure and a short. If your hearing isn't good, you can always check to see if the power supply fan is creating a breeze. Monitors are powered independently, so unless you're looking at a notebook PC, a live screen doesn't indicate a working power supply.

If the power doesn't come on, the first thing to check is that you have a live power source. You don't need a DVM (Digital Volt Meter) to check if your power outlet is live. Just unplug the power supply cord and plug in a lamp or a radio. If you are using a power strip, don't assume the socket you are using is good because the other outlets are working and the power strip status light is on. Many power strips I've encountered in the field have at least one bad outlet, and working outlets have been known to fail for no particularly good reason. Power supply cords very rarely fail, but it's possible for the female connector on the power supply end to back out of the socket. Make sure that both ends of the power supply cord are fully seated in the outlet and the power supply, respectively.

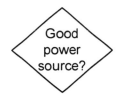

Check to make sure the correct voltage (110V/ 220V) is selected on the power supply. While this should never come up with a PC that's just been sitting on the desk, if you've replaced the power supply or moved the PC, it's always a possibility. This small red slide switch is located on power supply, usually between the power cord and the on/off override switch on the back of the case. Unplug the supply and select the proper voltage for your country. If you tried to power up with the switch set to 220V in a country using 110V, the system should be OK when you correct the voltage. If you tried running on 110V in a 220V country, you've probably blown a fuse in the supply (at the least), or damaged the supply and possibly other components.

If pressing your power switch doesn't immediately shut down the PC, that's normal for ATX systems. The action of the power switch is programmable and is controlled through CMOS Setup. The default operation for most power switches requires you to hold the switch in for three to five seconds before the system will power down. This allows use of the power switch to wake the PC from some power saving "sleep" or "stand-by" modes, depending on CMOS Setup power management settings. If the problem is that the operating system can't

turn off the PC when you shut down, it's likely a bad setting in power management or a corrupted file in the operating system.

One very good reason for the power supply to fail is an unconnected power switch. The power switch lead on ATX PCs, often labeled PW or PW-ON, runs from the front panel of the case to a connector block on the motherboard. This issue should only come up if you've been working in the case (the leads can pull off the connection block very easily), or if you've replaced the motherboard. The switch isn't polarized so it doesn't matter which way it goes on the motherboard posts, but it must be on the correct two posts. The proper location is usually printed right on the motherboard next to the connector block, and you can also consult the motherboard documentation. In cases where the documentation provided with the system and the information printed on the motherboard don't agree, I go with the motherboard.

Power switch fail?

Check the switch operation with a Digital Volt Meter on the continuity or resistance setting. On all ATX systems, the power switch is really just a logic switch that tells the motherboard, to which a trickle of live power is always supplied, to instruct the power supply to come fully alive. If your power supply features a heavy cord running forward to a large switch on the case front, with four connections, you have an old AT style supply and potentially deadly live line voltage is present at the switch. These procedures do not apply to the obsolete AT power supplies. When I'm working on an ATX system and don't have a tester handy, I short the two pins on the motherboard with a screwdriver, where the logic switch from front panel should be attached, and see if the system starts. This is a "live power" test. Don't do it if you may get startled and bash the screwdriver into something should the system power up, because there's no way to repair short-circuit or gouging damage once it's done. If the switch is bad and you don't have a replacement switch, check for a reset button on the front panel. You can usually get away with using the reset button for the PW-ON logic switch, and live without the hard reset.

Power supply connections to motherboard correct?

The power supply will to fail to operate if the power to motherboard isn't connected. Check that the 20 or 24 pin main ATX power connector and any additional motherboard power connections, such as the 4 pin ATX 12V supply (8 pin on some systems), are properly connected and seated. The latching mechanism for the standard ATX connector is counter-intuitive. You have to push in on the latch at the top to release it at the bottom, at which point the connector should pull off with almost no force required. You should hear or feel the latch click in when the connector is seated.

Remove the power leads to the drives to ensure that you aren't trying to power up into a short. The motherboard power must remain connected to activate the ATX power supply. If you have a DVM (Digital Volt Meter) and experience working around live circuitry, you can try checking the DC voltages at the connectors to see if they are live, or within 5% of the rated voltage. I'm not advising you do this live testing, as it's much easier and safer to try swapping in a new power supply. Unless you have a special testing fixture, you must leave the connectors attached while checking, which requires an exposed connector surface or a cheater lead. This is necessary because switching power supplies won't operate properly without a load, either failing to come on or even self-destructing (in extreme, low quality, instances). I just poke the DVM probes into the top of the 24 wire connector at the motherboard, since there's usually room next to the wire to get down to the conductor.

ATX Version 2.2 - 24 wire motherboard connector

Pin 1	Pin 2	Pin 3	Pin 4	Pin 5	Pin 6	Pin 7	Pin 8	Pin 9	Pin 10	Pin 11	Pin 12
3.3 V	3.3V	Gnd	5V	Gnd	5V	Gnd	P _ O K	5VSB	12V	12V	3.3V
Oran	Oran	Blk	Red	Blk	Red	Blk	Gray	Purp	Yell	Yell	Oran
Oran	Blue	Blk	Green	Blk	Blk	Blk	White	Red	Red	Red	Blk
3.3V	-12V	Gnd	P_ON	Gnd	Gnd	Gnd	-5V	5V	5V	5V	Gnd
Pin 13	Pin 14	Pin 15	Pin 16	Pin 17	Pin 18	Pin 19	Pin 20	Pin 21	Pin 22	Pin 23	Pin 24

The color scheme used for the voltages in the 24 pin connector holds for the other ATX standard power supply connectors. However, brand name manufacturers, especially older Dells, often used proprietary power supplies and made up their own color coding, so I wouldn't throw out a power supply that supplies 5V where you think it should supply 3.3V. It's more likely a proprietary design than a failure.

The 5V on Pin 9 is always present when the power supply is plugged in. This connection supplies power to the various PC circuits that operate even when the PC is turned off, such as "Wake on Modem" or "Wake on LAN." It's also the reason you should never work in the PC with the power supply plugged in, unless you can remember to turn off the override switch every time. This live power is supplied to the adapter slots, so replacing adapters with the power cord plugged in may damage the motherboard or adapters. Even though the drive leads aren't powered with the system turned off, you might drop a screw while working on a drive. If that screw lands in just the wrong place, like an open bus slot, it could create a short and damage the motherboard.

Assuming your PC is connected to a monitor, the next question is, do you have a live screen? Does text or a splash screen appear? A message saying "Please connect monitor" or "No video signal detected" counts as a "No" answer in this case. If the screen is live, but you see multiple images or endless scrolling, the video adapter is providing signals that cannot be interpreted by the monitor. This usually occurs when you attach an old monitor to a new PC and the monitor doesn't support the refresh rate at the screen resolution selected in the Windows settings.

Newer components like quad core processors and dual PCI Express video adapters have doubled the power requirements of typical gaming PCs. An entry level ATX power supply for a PCI Express gaming PC these days is 600W, and power supplies ranging from 750W to 1000W are no longer unusual. The primary culprits are multi-core CPUs that can consume anywhere from 10W to 50W or more per core, for a total CPU consumption as high as 200W in a single processor system. Meanwhile, PCI Express graphics cards for gaming can pull as much as 200 Watts by themselves, or double that in a dual card configuration.

While PC power supply manufacturers boast about their power rating, as it's their main selling point, manufacturers of video cards and other components don't trumpet their power consumption. You may have to do a little math to work it out. Sometimes they give the peak current requirement in Amps (A) at the supply voltage, usually 12V, so you multiply the two numbers for the power consumption in Watts. All of the high end video cards require more power than can be supplied through the PCI Express slot on the motherboard, so they are fed directly from the power supply with one or two 6-pin PCI Express supplementary connectors, or standard 4-pin Molex connectors, the kind used for non-SATA drives.

If the power supply comes on but you don't get a live screen, switch off and try again. You may have to hold the power switch in for five or more seconds before the system powers back down. If it fails to power down, you can turn off the switch on the back of the power supply, turn off your power strip, or unplug the cord. A PC that boots on the second or third try is most likely suffering from a quick power_ok (or power_good) signal, coming on before the power supply has stabilized. The presence of the power_ok signal tells the motherboard that the power supply is stable, while its absence tells the motherboard to stay off to protect itself. It's possible the power supply isn't quite up to the current ATX standard or the motherboard is a little too demanding about timing. Booting twice every time you want to turn on the PC isn't an ideal situation, so unless you leave it on all the time, look into buying a higher quality power supply, ideally one recommended by the motherboard manufacturer.

Beep codes are part of the PC's Power On Self Test (POST) routine. One beep means the system has passed the test and the BIOS believes that the CPU and memory and video are functioning properly. All other beep codes vary by BIOS supplier and system brand, but endlessly repeating slow beeps often indicate RAM failure, so shut down and try reseating the memory module(s). A repeated string of beeps, either 3 or 9 beeps long, is frequently video failure, so unplug the power and try reseating the video adapter. If you are getting beeps with a live screen, the problem is unlikely to be power supply related. Proceed to the Motherboard, CPU and RAM Failure diagnostics.

If you don't get any beeps, make sure the case speaker is connected and check for beeps again. If the motherboard lacks a connection point for a case speaker near the power switch and LED block, it probably employs an onboard piezoelectric speaker. If you have recently added any new components to the system, they may be overtaxing the power supply or causing a short circuit. This includes both adapters and drives. The first step in any failure situation is to try undoing the last change you made. I once encountered a system which powered up but failed to initialize the video adapter when the secondary IDE ribbon cable was connected backwards to a CD drive! Although the component you just added may have worked in another system, it doesn't mean you hooked it up properly, that it's compatible with the current PC, or that it didn't fail in the interim.

Common power supply problems unrelated to the boot process are noisy operation and unstable voltages, both of which are a reason to replace the supply. There are two common noise problems associated with power supplies, noisy fans and whistling capacitors. Noisy fans can be replaced, but only if you're a reasonably competent technician because you can really get a nasty zap from the stored energy in the capacitors even when the power supply is unplugged. Make sure your noisy fan problem isn't due to something silly like a piece of paper poking in through the fan grille before you rush out and buy a replacement. If your dog won't stay in the room when the computer is turned on or if your kids hear a high pitched whistling that you don't, it's probably a capacitor. To determine whether the capacitor is in the power supply or elsewhere in the system will require a process of elimination or some parts swapping.

Illustrated ATX power supply replacement:

www.fonerbooks.com /r_power.htm

Unstable voltage problems are real ghosts in the machine, and can mimic all sorts of other problems. If you get into a flaky failure situation that you can't diagnose and you've already started troubleshooting (i.e. swapping parts), you may as well try a new power supply as well. I've seen power supplies produce some really bizarre failures, like a PC that reboots when you set your coffee cup down too hard on the table. The most pervasive of the unstable power supply problems are random lockups or spontaneous reboots. Modern motherboards have some ability to regulate the power they receive, but it's got to be within a reasonable range. When it starts overshooting the limits, the system may freeze or shutdown the motherboard to protect itself.

As soon as the PC powers up, you should be able to hear the hard drive motor spin the drive (like a very, very, quiet jet taking off) and the read/write head seeking (a gentle clunking sound). If you're absolutely baffled as to whether or not the drive is spinning up, due to background noise or hearing problems, you can resort to feeling the drive cover. If that still doesn't do it, I power down, remove the drive cage or the drive itself, and hold it firmly by the edges (not touching any exposed wires or the circuit board on the bottom) while powering up. The drive resists twisting movements like a gyroscope if it's spun up. Don't play with it. If you move too fast or touch the circuit board to something that can cause a short, you'll damage the drive. Just power down, reinstall, and continue with the diagnostics.

If system power is coming on but the drive still isn't spinning up, make sure that your power lead is seated in the drive power socket. The old fashioned Molex connectors on pre-SATA drives should go in a good half inch or so. It does take a good deal of force to seat the cheaper leads in some drives. Try another lead, even if you have to disconnect another drive to get it. Try another drive. At this point it's still quite possible that the power supply is defective, but if you have a drive that you know spins up, it's a good way to eliminate one possibility. As long as you don't smell smoke coming out of the drive you can test the drive in another system. If you are using SCSI rather than IDE hard drives, check the documentation for a jumper that suppresses spin up on boot. SCSI drives offer this option because you can install as many as 15 in a single system, and if they all tried to spin up at once it would swamp any power supply. Normally, the SCSI host adapter will spin them up in order of their SCSI ID.

If system power isn't coming on, disconnect all drives, one at a time, and try powering up after each change. If the system powers up, you've found a faulty drive or a faulty lead from the power supply. If all of the SATA power connectors are dead, you can try running an SATA drive with an adapter on an old 4 pin Molex connector, or vise versa. If the system won't power up with all drives disconnected, start removing adapters, one at a time, leaving the video for last. Unplug

power cord before removing each adapter, then reconnect to power up.
If the system powers up, replace all adapters except the last one
removed before power came on. If power still comes on, try the last
adapter you removed in different slot before giving up on it.

If you find an adapter that actually prevents the system from powering
up, it must be replaced. If you are running with dual PCI Express
video cards, try running with just one and then just the other. If you
have a single video card slot, whether PCI Express or AGP, it could be
that slot is faulty. Another possibility is that the adapter is keyed as
universal but is installed on a new motherboard that expects low
voltage AGP adapters (AGP 4X or 8X).

Once you've eliminated the drives and the adapters, one of the few
remaining possibilities is a motherboard short. Remove the
motherboard and check for a standoff or screw located in the wrong
place or rolling around loose. I often build out systems on the bench
without a case, supporting the motherboard on a static proof bag over a
cardboard box or some similar arrangement to give the adapters room
to seat. This method eliminates any case mounting issues from the
diagnostics process, but it introduces all sorts of risks, not the least of
which is absence of the case ground.

Normally, a short circuit will result in a burnt smell and a ruined
motherboard, sometimes damaging any of the attached components
(memory, CPU, adapters) as well. In many instances, you'll be able to
figure out which component is ruined by the presence of burn marks or
a strong odor of smoke coming from the component, though if it
happens in a closed case, the smoky smell can stick to everything. If
you can't locate a failed component by visual inspection, you need to
have access to a test-bed system (an inexpensive but completely
functioning PC for testing questionable parts). Don't test parts that may
be fried in a good system, because some types of failures will cause
damage to the next machine.

If you've reached this point without getting the system to power up,
you probably have a defective power supply or motherboard. Try
replacing the power supply first since they're cheaper than
motherboards. Repairing power supplies requires a good knowledge of
electronics as there are usually "no user serviceable parts." Even when
power supplies are unplugged, they can give nasty zap from stored
power in the electrolytic capacitors. If the power supply or
motherboard is new, they may be incompatible with one another due to
poor adherence to ATX standards or support for different generations
of the ATX standard

Video Failure

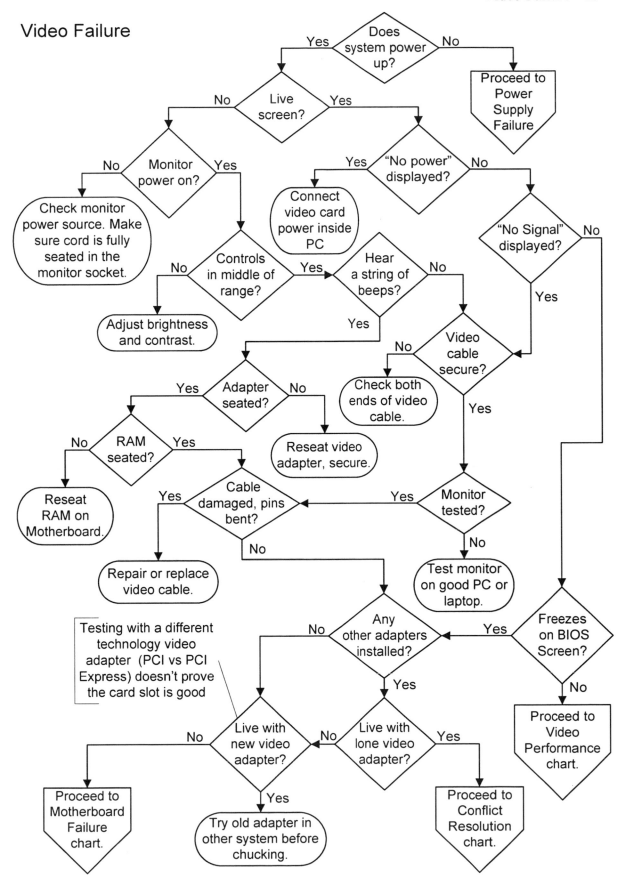

Video Failure

Is the system power coming on? Can you hear fans turning and drive motors spinning up, see little lights on the front of the CPU case, hear any beeps? We're talking about system power here, not the monitor power. If the system isn't powering up, or if you aren't sure whether or not it is, go to the Power Supply Failure chart now.

Does anything at all show up on the screen with the monitor power on, or is it just as black as before you powered on the CPU? We aren't demanding any signs of intelligent life in this case, any sign of life will do.

Assuming the system power comes up, does the monitor power come on? Monitors have a status LED on the front bezel that should show green, orange, or blinking if the monitor is powered on. You can also hear older monitors power on with a gentle sound, though I can't describe it beyond saying it's the sound of a CRT tube warming up. Make sure the monitor is plugged into a good outlet by testing the outlet with a lamp or any other device that will prove beyond a doubt that the outlet is good. Make sure that the power cord is either permanently attached at the monitor end or that it is seated fully in the socket, since partial cord insertion is the most common failure for monitors with detachable cords.

LCD displays don't make any sound when you turn them on, but they don't always have a simple power cord, either. Some LCD monitors are powered by an external transformer, which in turn is powered from a regular AC outlet. If the LCD display doesn't show any signs of life, make sure that the cords into and out of the transformer are fully seated. Some transformers are equipped with a status LED to show when they are operating, though you can also check for live output with a DC voltmeter. The power connection to the LCD display is often awkward to inspect, recessed into the back of the display. The important thing is to make sure it is started correctly, then seat it all the way.

Few things related to computers are more embarrassing than taking your monitor for repair and finding out that the brightness was turned all the way down. This frequently happens with exposed dials when you pick up the monitor and move it, though a prankster might also turn down the settings when they're concealed behind a pop-out door right under the screen. Make sure that manual brightness and contrast controls on the monitor are set somewhere in the middle of their range, since it's not always obvious which way is maximum or minimum. If the monitor is alive, turning the brightness and contrast all the way up

will often result in the screen lighting up a little. The easiest way to check if the monitor is good is to simply attach it to another working PC.

If you see a message on the screen that includes "power" in it, like: "attach graphics card power", "no power to video adapter", etc, it means that you have a PCI Express or older AGP video card that requires more power than the motherboard can supply through the bus. This means you need to run a power cable directly from the power supply to the video adapter, inside the PC. If it's a new build, you may have forgotten or not seated the connector firmly. If it was a working PC, either the power supply lead has failed, the power supply itself has problems, the cable worked loose, or some hardware on the video card has failed.

Replacing an AGP video adapter

www.fonerbooks.com /r_video.htm

Earlier video cards that required additional power from the power supply usually took a Molex connector, the same 4 pin connector used to power non-SATA drives. Newer power supplies include one or two six pin PCI Express supplementary connectors designed for power hungry graphics cards. Some PCI Express cards, in the absence of a six pin supplementary lead, will accept two 4 pin Molex leads.

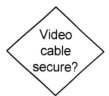

Most new monitors will display something such as "No signal source," or "Attach video signal," as long as they are healthy, and powered on. These messages should appear even if the PC or video adapter is dead. This is actually one of the more useful innovations in monitor technology, because it offers definitive proof that the monitor or LCD display is alive and most likely capable of displaying an image if a video signal was present. Unfortunately, it only proves something by its presence, since older monitors and cheaper models may not display anything at all.

Make sure the 15 pin video signal cable (3 rows of 5 pins each) is seated squarely on the video port on the back of the system. The hold-down screws on either side of the connector should be screwed in all the way, but not made up too tight. If the video cable is connected correctly, remove it and inspect the connector for damage.

Before making yourself nuts, test the monitor on another PC or laptop. If you use a laptop to test the monitor and it doesn't automatically detect an external monitor when booting, use the "F" function keys along the top of the keyboard to tell the laptop to shift to the external display. Remember that we are testing just to see if the monitor is live, it doesn't matter if the screen settings are wrong and the display looks funny. If it doesn't work on a known good computer, the problem is with the monitor, not your PC. If a faint image is detectable on an

LCD screen, the problem is with the backlight or the inverter that powers the backlight. A loud buzz coming from an LCD monitor is most likely the inverter circuit failing, though it can go on getting louder for years before it pops.

Look carefully at the pins in the connector to make sure none of them are at an angle or flattened against the bottom. Note that missing pins in a video cable are the norm, usually the monitor ID pins. It's great if you have a spare video cable and a monitor with a detachable cable, but most monitors have an integrated cable (doesn't detach) and most people don't have a spare anyway. You'll usually have to settle for visual inspection for whether the cable may have been crushed or breached.

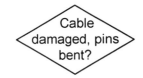

If you see that a pin in the connector is bent, you can try to straighten it very slowly with tweezers or fine needle nose pliers. If a pin breaks, you can buy a replacement connector and solder it on with a fine soldering iron and infinite patience. You'll also need a heatshrink gun and tubing if you want to do it right. The last time I did one it took me almost three hours, though I didn't really have the right soldering iron tip. I don't recommend making your own DVI connector.

Video Connector Pinout	8 - Blue Return (coax shield)
1 - Red	9 - No-Connection
2 - Green	10 - Sync Ground
3 - Blue	11 - Monitor ID
4 - Monitor ID (Note: pins for ID bits sometimes not present)	12 - Monitor ID
5 - Ground	13 - Horizontal-Sync
6 - Red Return (coax shield)	14 - Vertical-Sync
7 - Green Return (coax shield)	15 - Monitor ID

Do you hear a string of beeps? Healthy PCs should beep once or twice when they are turned on and pass their Power On Self Test (POST) routine. While different BIOS manufacturers use different beep codes to identify failures, a repeating string of beeps (three or nine in a row) is a common indicator of video card failure.

Check whether or not the video adapter is properly seated. This is an in-the-box check, so make sure you unplug the power cord to the system first. This doesn't apply to motherboards with built-in video. Whether or not the video adapter appears to be seated properly, reseat it. Remove the video adapter hold-down screw, remove the adapter, then reseat it in the slot, pushing down evenly. Be careful that putting the hold-down screw back in doesn't lever the front edge of the video adapter (the end away from the screw) up a fraction of an inch out of the slot, because that's all it takes if there's no hold-down latch.

If reseating the card doesn't clear up the beeps, it's probably a failed video adapter or RAM on the motherboard. You can power down and try reseating the RAM at this point, without going all the way through the motherboard diagnostics. There used to be beep codes for all sorts of component failures, but most of those components have long since been integrated into the motherboard and can't be replaced if they fail.

Does the system get as far as showing the BIOS screen and locking up? By BIOS screen, we're talking about the text information or brand-name graphics that appear on the screen in the initial boot stages. A system that freezes up at this point is rarely suffering from a video failure, though a conflict between the video card and another installed adapter is still possible.

Did you install any new adapters immediately before the problem appeared? With the power disconnected, remove any other adapters, one at a time, then reconnect power and attempt to reboot after each removal. Locking up on the BIOS screen is often due to an adapter conflict, but if removing the other adapters doesn't solve the problem, proceed to Motherboard, CPU and RAM Failure.

Do you get a live screen, or at least move past the BIOS screen, with all the other adapters removed? If so, the problem is either a bad adapter preventing proper operation of the bus or an adapter conflicting with the video card. In either case, you can reinstall the adapters one at a time, powering up after each one, troubleshooting the problem by process of elimination. Don't forget to unplug the system each time before taking any action inside the case.

If the motherboard is a new upgrade, try the video adapter in another system before trashing it, since it could be a simple incompatibility. If installing a new video adapter doesn't solve your "dead screen" problem, it's probably a motherboard related problem, even though you got to this point without any beep codes. Proceed to Motherboard, CPU and RAM Failure.

Video Performance

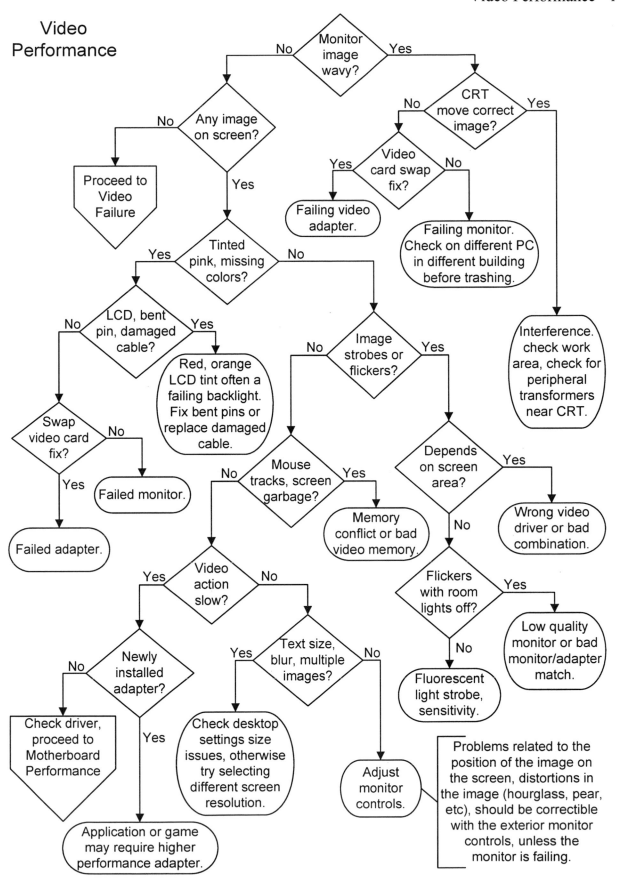

Video Performance

Is the image wavy, contorting in a regular manner, or is there scan line interference? The most common source of a wavy CRT image is magnetic interference, usually from a small transformer located right below or above the monitor, like the power supply for an inkjet or other peripheral device. Other image distortions and scan lines can be due an active RF source, like a radio transmitter, a wireless phone, or heavy duty currents flowing in nearby wall wiring.

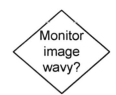

Try moving the whole system, CRT and all, well away from its current location. If you're in an industrial setting, try another building altogether. In a home environment, another room should be a fair test, but don't drag along the power transformer for the inkjet, which could be the source. However, if the screen shrinks and expands in a regular manner, beware of electricity supplied by large wind turbines in remote areas!

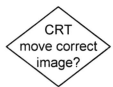

If moving the whole system doesn't correct an apparent interference problem, it's likely the monitor or the video adapter failing. Even though the monitor is the leading candidate, the best thing to do at this point is to test the monitor on another PC, simply because monitors are normally more expensive than video adapters. If you don't have access to any spare PCs or parts, I'd try a cheap old PCI adapter before investing in a new monitor.

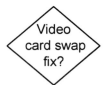

If you don't get any image at all, go back to the Video Failure chart. The following diagnostics all assume that the system is booting to the operating system and you're getting an image that fills the screen. Don't try making monitor adjustments on a text only screen or you may end up having to do it all over again.

Is the image correct, except the color is tinted pink or missing a primary color? It's not usual for a video cable to spontaneously fail on a working system, but inspect the cable for crushing and try a replacement if possible. With old CRT monitors, a missing color is either due to a failed gun, bad video cable or video adapter.

If the problem appeared immediately after moving the PC or changing monitors, you've probably crushed a pin in the 15 pin connector or the cable simply isn't seated all the way. A sudden color change is frequently a sign that you didn't screw in the connector thumb-screws, and it's falling off the port on the video card. With LCDs, a reddish/orange tint is a sign of a failing backlight.

Although this sort of failure normally suggests a failing monitor, particularly if it gets worse over time, you should always try the monitor on another PC before taking it to the dump. If you have a spare video card around (even if it's obsolete, as long as it works in your system), you can find out if the monitor is good. There are oddball video card failures that can duplicate monitor electronics problems.

Do you have the feeling that somebody is trying to sell you something through subliminal advertising? Try looking at the screen out of the corner of your eye, because peripheral vision is more sensitive to rapid movements. The most common reason for a flickering display is that the screen resolution is set too high for the video adapter, forcing it to switch to a slower scan rate. When the opposite is true, if the video card is attempting to drive the monitor at a faster refresh rate than it's capable of, you'll usually see multiple images or interference patterns on the screen, and a low quality monitor may even damage itself in trying to keep up.

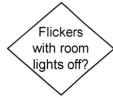

If lowering the screen resolution doesn't help, make sure you have the correct version of the video driver software installed. Try a different setting for the screen resolution and the number of colors. Make sure that hardware acceleration in Windows or any other operating system is turned on. Check the BIOS (CMOS Setup) to make sure that video BIOS caching is turned on (the default setting).

You can hit some combinations of room lighting and monitor frequencies that will cause a strobing effect to which some people are sensitive. Try operating with the lights turned off. If that cures the problem, try a different screen resolution which should produce a different vertical refresh rate. Some people are sensitive to fluorescent lights, even if there's nothing wrong with the video. Also keep in mind that monitors are designed for viewing from a distance of 18 inches, give or take a foot. Monitor images frequently look jumpy from across the room, but appear rock solid from the normal viewing distance.

Does your mouse leave tracks (droppings, really) on the screen, or do other screen images seem to refuse to give way to new information? The video memory on the adapter could be the culprit, though in most cases, this means trying another video card. A conflict with another adapter on the bus is also a possibility; check by removing all the other adapters. External interference is another possibility, I've heard of wireless phone usage causing this problem. As in all video problem cases, you should install the latest version of the video driver before giving up on the adapter.

Do windows move in a jerky fashion when you drag them around, is game performance poor, or do images seem to be painted on the screen one line at a time? Slow video action can be due to a number of related performance issues, such as available system memory, CPU speed, virtual memory setting, viruses, etc. From the standpoint of the video adapter, make sure hardware acceleration is enabled in Windows and that the most recent video driver for the adapter is installed. If hardware acceleration is enabled, try turning it off to see if it's a compatibility issue. If your video speed is fine in normal applications but gets jerky in some games, the adapter may not be 3D capable.

Did you recently install a new adapter or program? When in doubt, rip it out! There could be a bus contention problem if your video adapter is an older PCI model. New software can cause all sorts of unanticipated results, which is why there's an "Uninstall" option in Window Control Panel. Don't waste a lot of time worrying about how the change you just made could possibly affect the video performance, just find out if it did.

If the size of the icons on your screen changes, or the text under the icons or in the menus looks different than you remember, it's a desktop setting unrelated to hardware or drivers. It's easy to accidentally change these basic setting when you access a drop down menu with the pointer and click on an unintended option. If the problem is that everything is too large and blurry, or everything is too small, even to the extent of multiple copies of the same screen appearing side by side, the problem is a resolution mismatch between the monitor and the video driver. Try selecting a different resolution for the screen.

Is the image distorted but steady? Maybe shaped like an hourglass or a pear? Shifted to one side of the screen or the other? Too dim? Are the black areas are too bright? The problem is the monitor adjustments. Most of the monitor adjustments intended for user control are located under the screen (often behind a pop-out panel), or along the edges of the screen on the back. Occasionally they are found all the way on the back of the monitor at the bottom. If adjusting the controls outside the monitor doesn't fix the problem, you're probably out of luck, because the internal settings are tweaked at the factory.

CRT monitors contain lethal voltages and can kick you across the room with a capacitive shock even when they're turned off. You don't want to fiddle with adjustment pots inside a monitor if you haven't been trained. Technicians use a thin plastic (non-conductive blade) screwdriver for adjusting pots on live monitors. If you look carefully through the sides and back of the monitor with a flashlight, you may see some adjustable pots that can be diddled, but at best I've gained a couple months of sub-par operation through doing this. It's also possible to lose sync or ruin the color balance and have trouble getting back to the starting point. Don't even try this unless you're all paid up on your life insurance and the spouse is tired of you.

Motherboard, CPU, RAM Failure

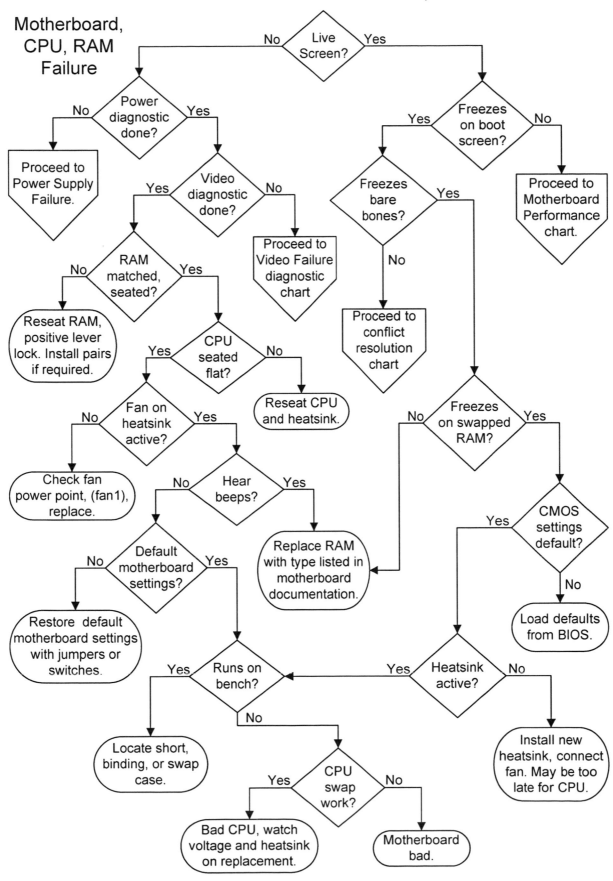

Motherboard, RAM, CPU Failure

Do you get a live screen? A message saying "No Video Signal" or anything similar doesn't count as a live screen in this case. You need to get at least as far as a BIOS screen, either the system BIOS or an adapter BIOS loading.

Does the system power up? Do you hear any beeps, drives spinning up, fans, etc. If the power isn't coming on, proceed to Power Supply Failure. If the power supply diagnostics sent you back here, follow through these diagnostics as a double-check before giving up on the motherboard.

If you haven't performed the Video Failure diagnostics for a dead screen yet, do so now. Don't ignore the obvious steps, like checking the power cord and the outlet. If you skip the video diagnostics and continue with the motherboard flowchart, you could easily end up buying replacement parts for hardware that's not bad.

One of the most common failures following motherboard or RAM upgrades is improper insertion of memory modules. The levers should be lowered before inserting the memory module, and should raise themselves up and lock in place when the module is correctly seated. If you're using obsolete RIMM (Rambus Inline Memory Module) memory, the modules in a bank must be matched, and you must install CRIMMs (Continuity RIMMs) in the empty sockets. If you're using older SIMM (Single Inline Memory Modules), each bank needs a matched pair. In both cases, matched doesn't just mean capacity and speed, it also means manufacturer.

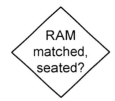

There are a number of reasons for a system with a good power supply to refuse to power up which were covered in the power supply diagnostics. Another reason is a failed CPU insertion, whether it's a slot or socket CPU. With good lighting, using a flashlight if necessary, make sure that any socket CPU is sitting dead flat in the socket, which means that the heatsink should be perfectly parallel to the motherboard surface; the CPU may be so totally hidden beneath some heatsinks that you can't see the edges. This problem should really only be relevant if you just upgraded your CPU or installed a new motherboard, because the CPU socket locks the CPU in firmly and the heatsink adds another level of clamping. If a socket CPU is a new install, you have to remove the heatsink and CPU to visually inspect it for damage such as crushed or bent legs. A CPU will not seat correctly if the socket locking arm wasn't raised all the way up before the CPU was inserted, or wasn't lowered all the way down after. If your CPU won't sit down in the socket properly, either the socket is faulty or you have the wrong CPU

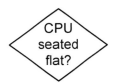

Illustrated CPU replacement:

www.fonerbooks.com /r_cpu.htm

for the motherboard! I haven't seen a CPU creep out of a socket due to thermal shock for over a decade.

It's pretty tough to tell if old slot type CPUs are seated by visual inspection, so when in doubt, I reseat them. On the plus side, you can remove and reseat a slot CPU without removing the heatsink, since they form an integral unit. Make sure you correctly identify release levers on a slot CPU package, which are normally located at the top of the CPU package, to the inside of the motherboard support structure.

A stone dead CPU is another reason for a system to fail. All modern CPUs require a heatsink, and most of these are an active heatsink, with a fan on top. You may encounter a heatsink without a fan in mass-manufactured brand-name systems where the manufacturer had the engineering talent in-house to do a thorough thermal analysis and determined that the airflow over a passive finned heatsink was enough to keep the CPU within the operating temperature range. When there is a fan on the heatsink, it must be hooked up to the correct power point on the motherboard for the BIOS to monitor its condition and turn it off and on. If you just installed a new CPU and powered the system up with no heatsink, it may have failed already. If the fan on your active heatsink isn't spinning up, replace it and hope for the best. Make sure you see the new heatsink fan operating since it could be the power point on the motherboard that's failed.

If you have a system that powers up, the next question is, do you hear any beeps coming from the motherboard speaker. If your motherboard doesn't have an integrated piezoelectric speaker but does have a speaker connection next to the power and reset connections (usually the front, left-hand corner of the motherboard) attach a case speaker. If you hear an unending string of beeps, it's often bad RAM, while a repeated sequence can be RAM or video. Other beep codes have been largely abandoned since they pertained to non-user replaceable surface mount components. Beeps or no beeps, I always reseat the video adapter and the RAM, paying special attention to the locking levers on the memory sockets.

Are your motherboard settings on the defaults? Whether you just put in a new motherboard or have been fooling around with overclocking, restore the default settings. This is often accomplished with a single jumper or switch setting, but sometimes it involves moving several jumpers or switches. Get the default values from the motherboard documentation. If you can't find the original manual or locate the equivalent documentation on the Internet, you may have to skip this procedure. Sometimes, the silk screens on the motherboard are sufficiently detailed to work out the defaults, but you need really good eyes to figure it out.

Although we're repeating a little of the power supply diagnostics here, stripping down the system is the next step in a "no power-up" scenario. Unplug the power cord before each change in the case. Disconnect drives, one at a time, reconnecting power and trying power up after each. Next start removing adapters, saving the video adapter for last, reconnecting power and retrying after each change to ensure you discover which component is causing the failure.

Running the motherboard without a case is a common technique used by technicians to eliminate any weird grounding and shorting issues or mechanical stresses. It also makes it much easier to swap the CPU if that's required. I normally do my bench testing on top of a cardboard box, with a static free bag or foam between the bottom of the motherboard and the cardboard. You don't walk away from a test like this or you might come back to find the box on fire! If your motherboard powers up on the bench with the same power supply that you used in the case, you have a geometry problem. Ideally, you should have a spare power supply for bench testing if you're going to do regular repair and testing work.

Make sure some standoffs aren't higher than others, putting unacceptable stress on the motherboard. Check that every standoff appears under a screw hole. The easiest way to be sure is to count the standoffs, count the screws, and make sure there are no screws leftover after you install the motherboard. There could be a short caused by a misplaced standoff, a loose screw, metal chips from shoddy materials. I've encountered standoff shorts that produce an endless string of beeps like RAM failure, without damaging the motherboard. There's also the possibility that the case geometry is so messed up (out of square or level when the cover is forced on) that it's putting an unacceptable mechanical stress on the motherboard resulting in an open circuit. If you can't find the cause of the problem, don't hesitate to try another case and power supply.

Illustrated motherboard installation:

www.fonerbooks.com /r_board.htm

If you still have a "no power" situation with the motherboard running out of the case, there's always the last refuge of a scoundrel. Swap in a known good CPU not forgetting to install a good heatsink and to connect the fan, even just for a quick test. I try to keep around some cheap old CPUs for this purpose, just in case the motherboard is a CPU eater. It's another good reason to leave all the motherboard settings on the default "Automatic" setting, so you don't have to fool around with them at this stage. If your old CPU is bad and the heatsink fan is dead, it's a pretty sure bet that the dead fan caused the CPU

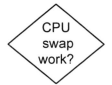

failure. If the heatsink fan is working, determining whether the CPU failure was due to poor heatsink contact, improper motherboard settings, or lousy power regulation from the motherboard is a guessing game. If the motherboard is an older make and you have a couple bucks to spare, replace the CPU and the motherboard together. Replacing just the CPU, even if the motherboard tests out OK, is kind of risky and usually tough to justify from a price/performance standpoint unless the system was practically new, say less than a half a year old.

Illustrated motherboard removal:

www.fonerbooks.com /r_mother.htm

If you still have a no power situation, not to mention no beeps and no video, you're probably looking at a bad motherboard. Again, this diagnosis assumes that you went through the Video Failure diagnostics, which would have forced you through the Power Supply Failure diagnostics as well. I still wouldn't be in a hurry to take a gun to the motherboard. Get your system operating with a replacement motherboard and all the identical parts that the old motherboard failed with before you make the trash can decision.

Freezes on boot screen?

Does the system power right up, give a happy beep or two, then freeze on the BIOS screen? This can occur on an all text screen, during or after memory count, while checking for drives, or the feared "Verifying DMI Data Pool." The problem is very likely due to a conflict, most like between the adapters but also possibly between incompatible drives sharing a bus.

Freezes bare bones?

Strip the system down to bare-bones, just a power supply, motherboard, minimum RAM, CPU and heatsink, and video adapter. If the system no longer freezes when it's stripped down, but complains about the lack of a boot device, proceed to Conflict Resolution.

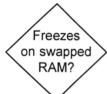

Freezes on swapped RAM?

Try swapping the RAM around, reordering the banks if you have more than one bank of RAM installed, or moving the only module installed to a neighboring slot. If this doesn't cure the freeze-up, and you have some suitable known good RAM from another system, try it. If the RAM currently installed doesn't meet the motherboard manufacturer specs, you shouldn't be using it; even if it seemed to work until this point. Improperly selected RAM can be the cause of problems ranging from no-boot to intermittent lock-ups. Is the RAM seated correctly and in the proper quantities (i.e., number of modules, addition of continuity modules, or CRIMMs, if you are using RIMMs). Also make sure that the system didn't use tinned (silver color) contacts against gold contacts, or the dissimilar metals will cause corrosion over time due to a constant electrical current when the power is off. Replacing RAM at this point isn't a guaranteed proposition, but it's a good item to eliminate. Don't toss out the RAM you remove because you may find out later that it's actually good.

If you aren't using the default CMOS settings, try restoring them all at this point. You can usually restore these from a major CMOS menu item like "Restore Default Settings" or "BIOS Default Settings." The default settings usually put everything on autodetect and use the recommended timing for the RAM. This means if you're overclocking, stop it, at least until you get the system running again. It doesn't matter whether or not overclocking the exact same CPU or RAM in a friend's system worked without a hitch, you're exceeding the manufacturers recommendations so it's a gamble.

An overheating CPU will cause the system to quickly lock up. Remove the existing heatsink and fan, make sure that the fan is working properly AND that the geometry of the bottom of the heatsink will bring it in full contact with the exposed CPU die or the top of the CPU package. Apply an approved thermal grease or thermal tape before reinstalling the heatsink. Don't put on too much thermal grease or you'll just make a mess. The thermal media is only there to fill the microscopic gaps between the die surface and the heatsink. Don't improvise your thermal material, go to a computer or electronics store and buy some. Installing heatsinks can be frustrating, but this isn't a "bash away at it" process. You can damage the CPU if you start cracking the heatsink against it in an attempt to get the heasink to sit right. Be patient, study the mechanical connections, make sure you aren't hitting some poorly placed component on the motherboard and check that your heatsink isn't so oversized it just won't fit on the particular motherboard.

Make sure the fan on that heatsink spins up the second that power comes on. If it doesn't, despite being connected to the correct power point (see the motherboard manual), replace it with a new active heatsink unit. Make sure the bottom surface of the new unit will make full contact with the exposed CPU die or the top of the CPU package. The only problem with replacing an active heatsink is it may be too late for your CPU. CPUs have an unfortunate tendency to damage themselves when they overheat. Some CPUs can go into thermal runaway and destroy themselves in a matter of seconds without proper cooling.

Motherboard, CPU, RAM Performance

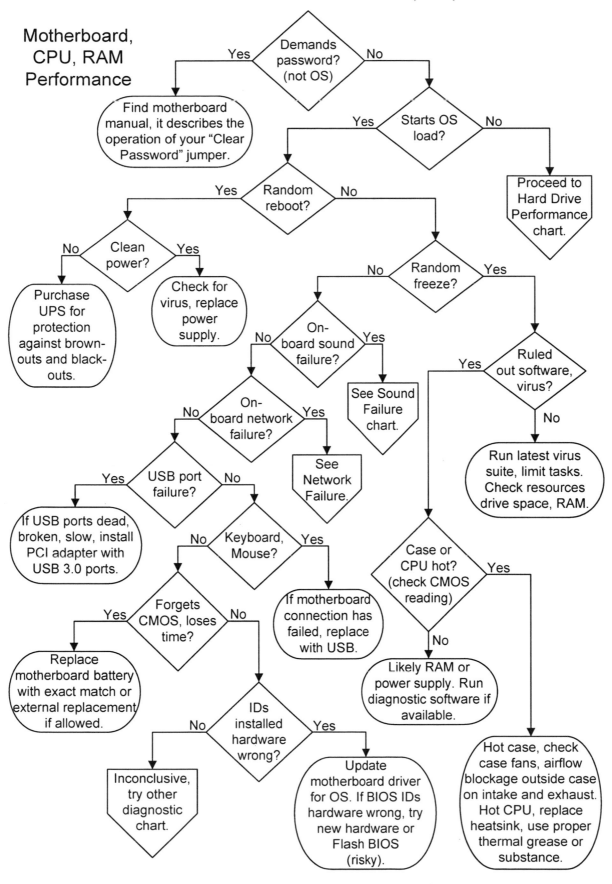

Demands password? (not OS)
- Yes → Find motherboard manual, it describes the operation of your "Clear Password" jumper.
- No → **Starts OS load?**
  - No → Proceed to Hard Drive Performance chart.
  - Yes → **Random reboot?**
    - Yes → **Clean power?**
      - No → Purchase UPS for protection against brown-outs and black-outs.
      - Yes → Check for virus, replace power supply.
    - No → **Random freeze?**
      - Yes → **Ruled out software, virus?**
        - Yes → **Case or CPU hot? (check CMOS reading)**
          - Yes → Hot case, check case fans, airflow blockage outside case on intake and exhaust. Hot CPU, replace heatsink, use proper thermal grease or substance.
          - No → Likely RAM or power supply. Run diagnostic software if available.
        - No → Run latest virus suite, limit tasks. Check resources drive space, RAM.
      - No → **On-board sound failure?**
        - Yes → See Sound Failure chart.
        - No → **On-board network failure?**
          - Yes → See Network Failure.
          - No → **USB port failure?**
            - Yes → If USB ports dead, broken, slow, install PCI adapter with USB 3.0 ports.
            - No → **Keyboard, Mouse?**
              - Yes → If motherboard connection has failed, replace with USB.
              - No → **Forgets CMOS, loses time?**
                - Yes → Replace motherboard battery with exact match or external replacement if allowed.
                - No → **IDs installed hardware wrong?**
                  - No → Inconclusive, try other diagnostic chart.
                  - Yes → Update motherboard driver for OS. If BIOS IDs hardware wrong, try new hardware or Flash BIOS (risky).

Motherboard, CPU, RAM Performance

Does your system power right up and demand a password? We're talking about pre-OS load here (a BIOS screen password), not a Windows password. This normally pops up in a small text box in the dead center of the screen, which usually is dark but for the box. If you don't know the password, you can try the BIOS manufacturer name (ie, AMI, AWARD, Phoenix) or the system brand name, but these are a long shot, since newer PCs don't allow a default password to be set. This screen means that somebody, maybe you, went into CMOS Setup and turned on Password Checking, normally found under the "Security" menu. Unfortunately, if the machine is asking for a password on boot, it will also demand a password to access Setup. Motherboards all come equipped with a "Forget Password" jumper, but you have to open up the case to get at it, so the usual precautions apply. Try to find the actual instruction manual, because the operation of these jumpers vary. Some want you to put the jumper on, power the system on and off quickly, and then put the jumper back in the default spot, some just want the jumper to be installed for a short time.

Does the system get as far as complaining about a missing boot drive, a bad disk, missing operating system, no boot partition, anything similar? If you get any of these messages, proceed to IDE Drive Failure diagnostics. If the system doesn't freeze on the BIOS screen, but doesn't start loading the OS either, it's unlikely a motherboard, CPU or RAM issue. If the system starts to load the OS and freezes in the same place every time, it's most likely an adapter conflict, so proceed to Conflict Resolution.

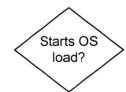

Does the system reboot itself for no apparent reason, either during the boot process or at any point once you're up and running? Random reboots are often caused by mechanical or thermal problems. However, keep in mind that a really silly power management setting may be sending your system into sleep mode after one minute of inactivity. A corrupted operating system or a virus can also cause repeated reboots, though a single startup in Safe Mode will normally cure the former.

I've seen bad power supplies that cause a system to reboot if somebody walks across the room or sets a coffee cup down on the table. I always try the swapping the power supply first with random reboots, but it could also be very bad (dirty, spiky) power in the building or an extreme case of interference. If your system reboots when you warm that coffee up in the microwave, I'd tend to worry about what the microwave is doing to you as well as to your computer!

Is your PC suffering from random lockups? We're talking about lockups that you need to use the reset button or power off and on to clear. If you can CRTL-ALT-DEL your way out of a lock-up, in fact, if you can get any response with it at all, it's more likely a software conflict or incompatibility.

Do yourself a favor and eliminate all possibility of software problems first. The easiest way to do this is to take out the hard drive, stick in a temporary hard drive, install an operating system and run it. If you still have lock-ups, you can start worrying about the hardware, otherwise it's a software issue. Well, it's also possible that the lockups were due to the old hard drive failing, but at least it eliminates the rest of the hardware from the equation. Although the CPU, RAM and motherboard are all candidates for intermittent lock-ups, the hard drive, the ribbon cables, and external interference are also possibilities.

You also want to monitor the heat in the system and in the room. If the problem first appeared during the summer or when the air-conditioning failed, it's probably heat related. The PC's ability to cool itself is entirely dependent on the outside air temperature being reasonable. If you run your server in a closet and the air in there gets up to 120 degrees, it would be a minor miracle if it didn't suffer from random lockups.

Is your sound card a high end PCI adapter or integrated on the motherboard? If your problem is sound failure, you need to go through those diagnostics in any case, but if the problem turns out to be that the motherboard controller has failed, there's no point in replacing the motherboard. You can use either a high end PCI sound adapter, assuming you have an open slot, a USB sound card, which allows you to attach your old analog speakers and mic, or just buy USB speakers or a USB mic, which have their own built in sound capability.

Standard 100BaseT or 1000BaseT networking has been built into pretty much all motherboard I/O cores for the last decade plus a few years. If you go through the network failure diagnostics and conclude that the problem is your integrated network controller, you can replace it with a PCI adapter or a USB adapter. If it's for an in-home network and you have a wireless router, you also have the option of installing a cheap wireless card or wireless USB stub antenna.

Check the peripheral manual before you tear your computer apart trying to solve a blinking light on the Inkjet that's telling you about a paper jam. If the port is physically broken on the motherboard, no longer shows up in Device Manager, or is too slow for your peripheral, you can install a PCI adapter with the latest USB 3.0 ports, as long as there's an empty expansion slot available on the motherboard. For printers, scanners, digital cameras, etc, proceed to Peripheral Failure diagnostics.

Has your PS/2 port for the keyboard or mouse stopped responding or broken off the motherboard? First, make sure you haven't confused the keyboard and mouse cables, since they use the same connector. They are normally color coded, green for mouse and purple for keyboard. If the port really is bad, just replace the mouse or keyboard with a USB mouse or keyboard, or buy a USB splitter for a few bucks that gives you two PS/2 connectors by way of a USB port.

Does the system clock keep time badly, or does the system ever enter CMOS Setup for no apparent reason, or even give you a "Low Battery" warning at boot (we're talking about desktop PCs here, not notebooks). Most motherboards have a replaceable battery likely to be a large watch type battery, though universal replacements for a given voltage are available. The battery really shouldn't fail during the usable life of the PC, say 4 or 5 years, and if it does, the problem may turn out to be that something is causing it to drain too quickly. If you find yourself replacing the battery every month, I wouldn't bother. I'd give up and live with the problem or swap the motherboard.

Does your motherboard identify installed components incorrectly? This includes CPU type and speed, memory quantity and speed, adapters and drives. There are three basic reasons for the motherboard to fail to recognize components properly:

> You've manually forced the wrong settings with motherboard jumpers or in CMOS
> The BIOS is old
> The components are too new for the motherboard and it's just not going to work

If you are overclocking, or if you have an old motherboard and simply set the jumpers wrong for the CPU or the RAM speed, the motherboard has every reason to identify them improperly. There are usually CMOS Setup options that allow you to change the ATA protocol and disable most of motherboard features. Before blaming the problems on an old BIOS, make sure you're using the default automatic settings on both the motherboard and in CMOS Setup. New motherboards are often jumperless, with all settings controlled through CMOS Setup or automatic configuration.

The only fix for an old BIOS is to flash it, to update the BIOS code with new code from the motherboard manufacturer. I've lost

Illustrated RAM
replacement:

www.fonerbooks.com
/r_ram.htm

motherboards trying to flash the BIOS. The procedure is simple, you download the software from the manufacturer's website and the process is automatic when you run the program, but BEWARE. If you grab the wrong version of the BIOS off the web, if the manufacturer has made a mistake, if you can't quite determine which revision of a motherboard you have, or if the process gets interrupted in the middle by a power spike, etc, you can lose the motherboard. In other words, if the BIOS doesn't get completely installed or isn't correct, you can never boot the system again to fix it and you're usually stuck buying a new motherboard or sending it out to the manufacturer, since BIOS chips are rarely socketed these days. For me, flashing the BIOS is a last resort.

It's also possible that the components you have installed are too new for the BIOS to know what to make of them. Sometimes the BIOS will identify the component correctly, like a CPU or a hard drive, but will operate it at the highest speed or capacity that the motherboard is capable of. This problem isn't anybody's fault, it's just not possible for motherboard manufacturers to be prepared for everything that may come down the pike in the next couple years. Not to mention testing compliance with hardware that doesn't exist yet.

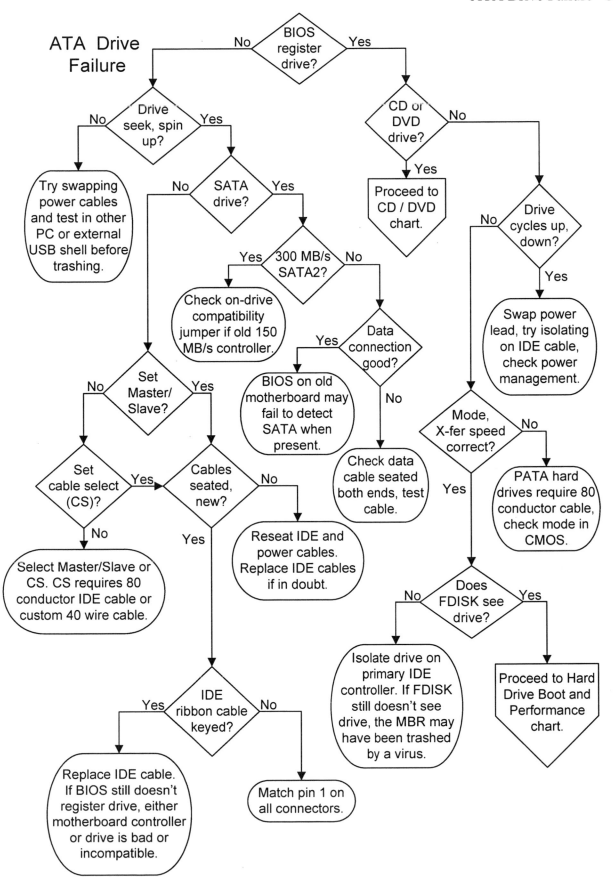

ATA Drive
Failure

BIOS register drive?

No → Drive seek, spin up?

No → Try swapping power cables and test in other PC or external USB shell before trashing.

Yes → SATA drive?

No → Set Master/Slave?

Yes → 300 MB/s SATA2?

Yes → Check on-drive compatibility jumper if old 150 MB/s controller.

No → Data connection good?

Yes → BIOS on old motherboard may fail to detect SATA when present.

No → Check data cable seated both ends, test cable.

Set Master/Slave?

No → Set cable select (CS)?

Yes → Cables seated, new?

No → Reseat IDE and power cables. Replace IDE cables if in doubt.

Yes → IDE ribbon cable keyed?

No → Select Master/Slave or CS. CS requires 80 conductor IDE cable or custom 40 wire cable.

Yes → Replace IDE cable. If BIOS still doesn't register drive, either motherboard controller or drive is bad or incompatible.

No → Match pin 1 on all connectors.

BIOS register drive? Yes → CD or DVD drive?

Yes → Proceed to CD / DVD chart.

No → Drive cycles up, down?

No → Mode, X-fer speed correct?

Yes → Swap power lead, try isolating on IDE cable, check power management.

Mode, X-fer speed correct?

No → PATA hard drives require 80 conductor cable, check mode in CMOS.

Yes → Does FDISK see drive?

No → Isolate drive on primary IDE controller. If FDISK still doesn't see drive, the MBR may have been trashed by a virus.

Yes → Proceed to Hard Drive Boot and Performance chart.

ATA Drive Failure

Are all installed ATA drives properly identified by the BIOS and displayed on the start-up screen? Any modern PC should be able to identify the drive by model number, brand, capacity, and usually the transfer mode. Some brand name PCs may not display a start-up BIOS registration screen, so you'll have to enter CMOS Setup to view the information. If the key stroke required to enter CMOS Setup isn't displayed on the screen as the PC begins to boot, you'll need to look it up in the documentation or on the Internet. Common keys used to access CMOS Setup at boot are, <DEL>, <F1> and <F2>.

Does the hard drive spin up? We covered this in the power supply diagnostics, but I'll repeat it here for convenience. When the PC powers up, you should hear the hard drive motor spinning up the drive and the gentle clunking sound of the read/wrote head seeking. If I can't tell whether or not the drive is spinning up, even with my fingers on the drive's top cover, I run the drive in my hand. A spun up drive resists a slow twisting movement just like a gyroscope. Don't flip it quickly or play with it or you may damage the drive, not to mention touching the circuitry against a conductor and causing a short. Just power down, put the drive back in and continue with the diagnostics. If it's a SCSI drive, you're on the wrong diagnostics page, but maybe some new ATA hard drive will adopt the SCSI practice of a jumper to delay spin up. SCSI drives offer this option since you can install up to 15 on a single controller, and spinning them all up at once would cause the hardiest power supply to droop. Try swapping the power lead or running the drive on another power supply. One of the reasons I always use four screws in older PATA drives is so I can push hard on the power connector without the unit shifting around and possibly damaging the circuit board. I've never broken a power socket off the circuit board on a hard drive, but I've seen it done, so don't go too crazy on it. Try the hard drive in another PC or a USB shell before you conclude that it's dead.

Illustrated PATA hard drive replacement:

www.fonerbooks.com /r_hard.htm

The diagnostic tree splits here between the newer SATA (Serial ATA) drives and the older PATA (Parallel ATA) drives. PATA drives are often referred to as plain "ATA" or "IDE", the terms refer to the same technology. SATA and PATA drives feature different connectors for both for power and data, so you can't hook the wrong drive up to the wrong interface. On the SATA drives, the power cable is wider than the data cable, on the older PATA or IDE drives, the data cable is a wide ribbon cable and the power cable is an old fashioned Molex with red, yellow and black wires.

The initial interface speed for SATA drives was 150 MB/s, also known as SATA 1. The newer 300 MB/s SATA 2 drives are now widely available, but replacing a SATA 1 hard drive with a SATA 2 hard drive on an older PC can get tricky. If the SATA 2 drive isn't recognized by the BIOS or won't boot reliably, check if the drive has an onboard compatibility jumper that will force it to work properly with the older 150 MB/s controller.

SATA drives are pretty bullet-proof in comparison with the older IDE technology. If the drive powers up but isn't recognized by the BIOS, it's possible that the data cable is bad, or not properly seated on either the drive and the motherboard. If the data cable is known to be good (ie, it works in another system), try attaching it to a different SATA port on the motherboard. Some motherboards offer a completely separate set of SATA connectors for RAID arrays (see hard drive performance). If the drive manufacturer supplied software that works with the drive and the operating system loads, even though the BIOS doesn't recognize the drive, you can still use it.

Any time two old IDE drives share a single cable, the computer needs a way to tell them apart. This can be accomplished by using jumpers on the drives to set one to "Master" and the other to "Slave" or through selection by the cable. The Master/Slave setting is fixed by a single jumper, usually on the back end of the drive between the power socket and the IDE connector. The labeling for the jumpers is usually in shorthand, "M" for Master and "S" for Slave. Some older drives include a jumper for "Single" (and spelled out labels) for when the drive is the only drive installed on the ribbon. Since pre-SATA motherboards always supported both a primary and a secondary IDE interface, it's not necessary with a two drive system to hang them both on the same cable. The boot hard drive should always be the Master on the primary IDE interface. If the CD, DVD, or any other IDE drive is to share the same cable, it should be set to Slave.

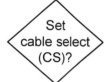

Most new PATA drives support Cable Select (CS) which means the pin 28 connection in the cable will determine which drive is Master and which is Slave. The 80 wire ribbon cables that should come with all new motherboards and drives support cables select and have color coded connectors: Motherboard IDE Connector - Blue, Slave IDE connector (middle connector on cable) - Grey, Master - Black. Cable select is supported by custom 40 wire ribbon cable and older drives; these are usually found in brand-name systems. The jumpers on both drives should be set to cable select if you aren't setting one as Master and the other as Slave.

If the drives still don't register properly, make sure the power cable is seated in the drive's power socket, which can take a bit of force. The ribbon cable connectors must also be seated all the way into the IDE port on both the drives and the motherboard, or adapter card if you're are using a RAID adapter. The most common reason for a cabling failure of this sort is that the connection was partially dislodged when you were working in the case on something else. Try a new ribbon cable. While cable failures are rare, it can happen, and it's a favorite trick of investigative reporters writing articles about computer repair rip-offs to intentionally introduce a bad IDE cable into a PC, just to see how many parts a shop will sell them.

Are the ribbon cable connectors and the IDE ports on the drives and the motherboard keyed such that the cable can only go one way? Check the pin 1 location on all of the connectors and ports. On IDE drives, pin 1 is traditionally located next to the power cord, but it's not a 100% rule for all time. Motherboards can be pretty strange about cable ports. I've even remember an old one where the pin numbering on the floppy and IDE interfaces were oriented in opposite directions. The pin 1 location on the motherboard is normally marked with an arrow, a dot, a white square, anything to show one end of the interface as different from the other. If the motherboard won't register any drive you attach, even on new cables, and if those drives are spinning up, it indicates that either the IDE controller is bad or all the drives you've tried are bad. You can try running on the secondary IDE controller if you've only been working with the primary, but the next stop is installing an add-in IDE adapter or replacing the motherboard.

The troubleshooting procedures for ATA drives that aren't recognized by the BIOS are identical, whether they are hard drives, CDs, DVDs, tapes or any other ATA device. If the BIOS registers the installed ATA drives correctly and the drive you're having problems with is a CD or DVD, proceed to the CD or DVD Failure diagnostics.

Does the drive cycle up and down? Try swapping the power lead for a spare or one used by another drive. For older IDE drives, try isolating the drive on its ribbon cable, even if it means temporarily doing without another drive for the sake of troubleshooting. If neither fix helps, try disconnecting the data cable to ensure that the drive isn't receiving some flaky power down signal from a bad ATA interface or crazy power management scheme. If it still cycles up and down, the drive is probably toast. Test the drive in another system or a USB shell before labeling it dead.

If you have an old drive that spins up but won't seek (you never hear the head move in and out), it's probably a mechanical failure. The last ditch effort before giving up or sending it out for data recovery is tapping lightly with a screwdriver on the cover of the drive, away from the circular section where the disks are spinning. This might encourage a stuck head to get moving. Freezing the drive for a few hours in the freezer (use a sealed bag) may get you temporary access to a drive with failing electronics that overheat in a hurry. Just make sure you have your backup media prepared if you try any of these last ditch efforts, because it may work just the one time.

Does the drive make little clicking noises and fail to get going? Restart the machine, with the reset button if you have one, and hopefully it will boot. If not, try in a warmer room, or put the PC in direct sunlight to warm up and then try it again. It's far from guaranteed, but this is one of the few problems that can result from the drive being too cold rather than too hot. If you do get it started, run ScanDisk. It doesn't hurt to reseat all of the cables on the drive and the ribbon cable to the motherboard, since connections can also loosen up over time. However, if you can't get it going, it could be a legitimate drive failure. If you don't mind losing all of the data onboard, try FDISKing and reinstalling the operating system again.

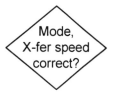

Does the BIOS report the transfer mode correctly for older PATA drives, ie, UDMA/100, ATA/66? UDMA must be enabled in CMOS, or set on "Auto," for high speed transfers. IDE hard drives after around 1995 require the 80 wire ribbon cable, at least for high speed operation. You can check CMOS Setup to see if there's a manual override to select the higher speed transfers, though the automatic settings should pick it up. Also try isolating the hard drive as the sole device on the primary controller. If you're adding a new hard drive to an older system, it's possible that the old motherboard and BIOS simply don't support the faster transfer, even with the new cable. I'd be leery of flashing the BIOS to try to get the speed up, even if the motherboard manufacturer supplies it.

Can you install an operating system, or access the drive with any generation of FDISK to create or view partitions? Check again that the ribbon cable is fully and evenly seated and there aren't any "read only" jumpers set on the drive (normally only found on SCSI's). Try a new ribbon cable. If this doesn't do it, it sounds like either the drive's MBR is messed up, or there's a problem with the way the software is communicating with the BIOS, which really shouldn't happen. If you don't mind losing whatever info is on the drive, you can try FDISK/MBR and see if it helps.

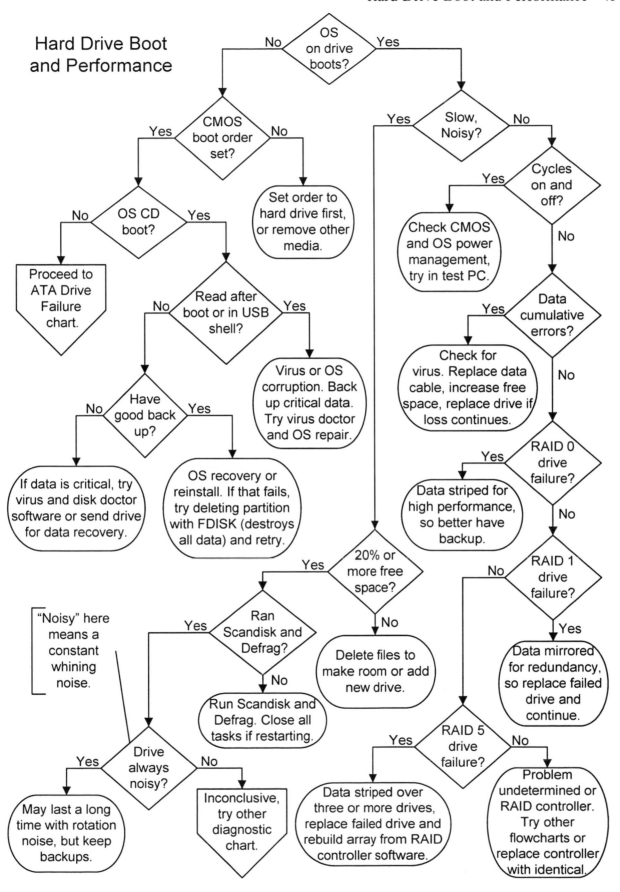

Hard Drive Boot and Performance

Hard Drive Boot and Performance

Do you get at least a partial operating system load? This includes the Windows splash screen, or even just the running dots when a kernel is loading. Has the drive been moved from another system? Retry booting in Safe Mode, since all the drivers for the underlying hardware will be incorrect in Windows. It's possible for a drive that's been moved from another system to begin booting even if the drive parameters and addressing mode have been detected wrong. Old PCs accepted manual input of hard drive parameters that can't always be detected by a new motherboard. Otherwise, boot failure is probably unrelated to the drive itself and due to a hardware conflict, data corruption, a bad install, etc. One good test is to boot from an operating system CD and run ScanDisk.

Have you checked the boot order of all the installed devices in CMOS Setup? The boot order specifies which drive should be tried first, and should be set to your boot hard drive unless you are having trouble with an operating system install. If you absolutely prefer to leave the DVD or the CD as the first boot device, remove any media from those drives. If the hard drive still fails to boot, set it to be the first boot device.

Can you boot an operating system DVD or CD? If not, this is where you change the boot order to try the CD first. If it still doesn't boot, it could be that the CD/DVD drive is taking too long to spin up and the BIOS is timing out. Try ejecting the disc, hitting the reset button on the PC, and then sliding the tray back in so that the drive will be spinning up by itself by the time the BIOS checks for a CD. Confirm that the CD is bootable in another PC, try wiping it off with a flannel shirt if it's covered with finger prints. If you can't get booted from either a hard drive with a known good operating system installed or a bootable operating system CD, it sounds like an ATA controller or cabling problem and you need to return to the ATA Failure chart.

After you've booted from an operating system CD, can you read the information on the hard drive? Can you read the drive data if it's installed in an external USB shell? If you can, the operating system has been corrupted. This could be due to a failed software upgrade, a virus, an actual error writing the hard drive, or a piece of software running amok and writing data to the wrong location on the drive. Back up any critical data while you can access the drive, then use the operating system CD to repair or reinstall (options depend on particular OS and PC manufacturer). Most operating systems allow you to reinstall without wiping out any of your data or programs. They

(should) always prompt you to see if you want to continue before actually destroying any data.

Do you have a good backup? A good backup doesn't just mean that the tape runs every night, it means that you've actually checked the tape to make sure that the files you need are on there and that you can access them. If you do have a good backup and the OS recovery has failed, you can try deleting the partitions on the drive with FDISK and starting from scratch. This means losing all of the information on your drive, so if you have any critical data and you aren't sure of what you're doing, seek professional help.

If you don't have a good backup and the data is critical, you might want to invest in the latest disk doctor and virus doctor software you can find. If the data is really critical, you can send the drive out to a data recovery outfit. Data recovery is expensive, from the mid-hundreds to thousands of dollars, but they can usually recover data from a drive as long as it hasn't been maliciously wiped out and the data platters haven't been physically damaged.

Is the drive slow (i.e., slower than it used to be or slower than you expected based on experience)? Is the drive noisy, either in terms of volume (i.e., "That's one loud drive") or simply because it never stops seeking? Some drives are pretty quiet even when they are constantly seeking, so if the hard drive status LED on the front of the computer blinks continually even after the operating system has finished loading and no software is running, count that as "noisy."

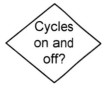

Does it seem to take forever to load a new file from the drive or to start a program? Can you actually hear the drive spinning up whenever you do something that requires drive access? It could just be that the power management settings for the drive are too aggressive and that either the operating system or the BIOS (through CMOS Setup) is telling the hard drive to power down any time you don't access it for 60 seconds. Turn off power management in CMOS Setup, at least for the hard drive, if that's an option. Check the power management settings in Windows Control Panel and turn off hard drive power management.

If you have two drives installed in a high performance gaming PC, there's a good chance you're running a RAID 0 array. This is true for both newer SATA and older PATA or IDE systems. Because RAID 0 stripes data across drives with no backup for the highest performance, if you lose one drive, you need to start from scratch because the remaining drive only holds data fragments. RAID arrays are generally accessed and maintained through a BIOS screen that can be

independent of than the main system BIOS, and accessed through
another key combination on start-up.

If you had two drives installed in your PC for the sake of data security,
then you are probably running a RAID 1 array. RAID 1 mirrors every
bit of data on both drives, so if one drive fails, the system should
inform you that it needs to be replaced but continue running as usual.
The problem is, many people confuse drive integrity with data
security. If you get a virus or other malware infestation, or if you
accidentally delete data, the deletion or infestation is mirrored to both
drives. The only true security is in incrementally backing up your data
and storing multiple copies offsite.

If you have three or more hard drives installed in a server, you're
probably running a RAID 5 configuration. RAID 5 employs both data
striping and parity (a form of error checking) so that in the case of a
single drive failure, the array can rebuild itself with no data loss when
the failed drive is replaced with an empty new drive. If you've reached
this point without seeing your hard drive performance issue, it's likely
a software problem or an OS compatibility problem with the
controller.

Does your drive accumulate data errors? Have you had to reinstall the
operating system more than once, or is ScanDisk constantly telling you
that it's recovering lost files? First, make sure at least 10% of the drive
capacity is unused (I shoot for 20% myself), then check for a virus.
Try running a "Thorough" scan with ScanDisk, which verifies the
physical disk surfaces and can take all night on a large hard drive. If
ScanDisk identifies physical errors on the drive, and the number
increases the next time you check, the drive is failing.

As always, check the IDE or SATA data cable, and if you've been
fooling around in the case quite a bit, it's worth a shot to replace it.
Check for viruses. Errors can result from the drive running too hot, so
if it's a hundred degrees in the room, consider air conditioning or
moving the PC. It can also get pretty hot in the case even in an air-
conditioned environment if there isn't enough air circulation in the
case and the drives are stacked in like pancakes. RF interference is
another (remote) possibility, from a poorly designed or partially failed
adapter on the bus that's acting like a broadcast antenna at just the
wrong frequency. Back up all of your data (really the first thing you
should do when you start seeing data errors on a drive) and reformat
the drive. Do a slow format, not the fast format some OS installs
allow. You know it's a slow format when it takes hours.

First make sure the drive isn't getting full. As a rule of thumb, I don't like to let a drive get more than 80% full, due to the demands of virtual memory and imaging requirements for burning DVDs and the like. Many programs create large temporary files without really documenting the fact, so you can be sure you always need more free space than you think.

Have you defragmented the disk recently? Run Defrag (in most Windows versions, this is found under Programs > Accessories > System Tools). If Defrag gives you any grief, run ScanDisk first (same location). If ScanDisk doesn't get through the drive, make sure you aren't running any other programs (you can often use crtl-alt-del to end all the non-critical tasks), and try again. If it still doesn't work, restart in Safe Mode and try. If you still can't get through ScanDisk, consider backing up your data and reformatting the drive. It's a tough call at this point, if you've defragged the drive, it's not full, and it's still slowly beating itself to death. Buy or download some decent virus doctor and spyware eradicator software, because you probably have a virus or a mess of spyware on the drive making life miserable.

If your drive is continually noisy, sounds like a quiet airplane as it spins up and then makes high pitched rotational noise all the time, it's just mechanical noise. While it's not a good sign, and I would suggest replacing the drive, I've also seen noisy hard drives linger for years and years. Another possibility, if your hard drive is slow, is that it's not the hard drive at all. Download some benchmarking software or use the Windows performance monitor to determine exactly where the bottleneck in your system is.

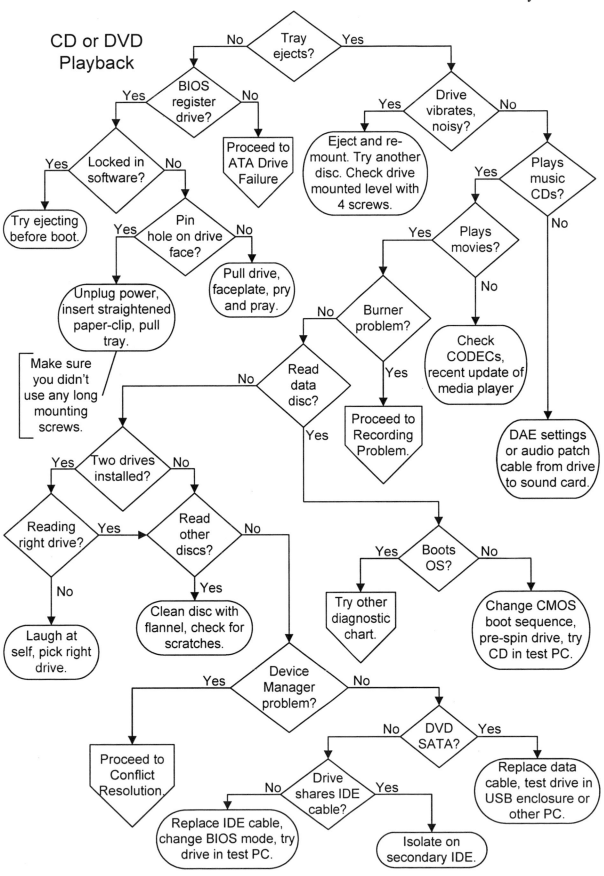

CD or DVD Playback

Tray ejects?
- No → **BIOS register drive?**
  - Yes → **Locked in software?**
    - Yes → Try ejecting before boot.
    - No → **Pin hole on drive face?**
      - Yes → Unplug power, insert straightened paper-clip, pull tray.
        - Make sure you didn't use any long mounting screws.
      - No → Pull drive, faceplate, pry and pray.
  - No → Proceed to ATA Drive Failure
- Yes → **Drive vibrates, noisy?**
  - Yes → Eject and re-mount. Try another disc. Check drive mounted level with 4 screws.
  - No → **Plays music CDs?**
    - Yes → **Plays movies?**
      - Yes → **Burner problem?**
        - No → **Read data disc?**
        - Yes → Proceed to Recording Problem.
      - No → Check CODECs, recent update of media player
    - No → DAE settings or audio patch cable from drive to sound card.

Read data disc?
- No → **Two drives installed?**
  - Yes → **Reading right drive?**
    - Yes → **Read other discs?**
    - No → Laugh at self, pick right drive.
  - No → **Read other discs?**
    - Yes → Clean disc with flannel, check for scratches.
    - No → **Device Manager problem?**
- Yes → **Boots OS?**
  - Yes → Try other diagnostic chart.
  - No → Change CMOS boot sequence, pre-spin drive, try CD in test PC.

Device Manager problem?
- Yes → Proceed to Conflict Resolution.
- No → **DVD SATA?**
  - No → **Drive shares IDE cable?**
    - No → Replace IDE cable, change BIOS mode, try drive in test PC.
    - Yes → Isolate on secondary IDE.
  - Yes → Replace data cable, test drive in USB enclosure or other PC.

CD or DVD Playback

The most basic and potentially most disastrous problem that can occur with a CD or DVD drive is a stuck tray. Will the tray eject when you press the eject button? Press it once, like a doorbell, and then move your finger away, or you may be sending it repeated open and close commands. The drive won't pop right open if it is actively playing a disc, and the operating system may be able to override the stop and open command. If you're trying to eject a music CD or DVD using Media Player software (clicking on a software eject button on the screen) and it doesn't work, try the manual button on the drive. If this is a newly installed drive, make sure you used the short screws shipped with the drive and not longer screws which can jam the mechanism. If there's a disc in the drive that can no longer be read, make sure the power supply lead is still seated in the socket on the back of the drive.

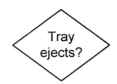

Shut down, restart, and try again. If the tray still doesn't eject, reboot again and note whether the BIOS registers the drive. Some brand name PCs don't report installed hardware on a boot screen, so you'll have to access CMOS Setup to check. If the BIOS doesn't registered the drive, it may have dropped dead. Proceed to ATA Drive Failure if the BIOS no longer registers the drive.

Before you start tearing apart the machine, make sure that the tray isn't locked by software. The easiest way to check is to reboot the PC and hit the eject button before the operating system loads, but you can also check the properties under the drive icon in Windows "My Computer." If the drive LED shows that it's trying to read a disc, and the eject button doesn't interrupt the task, it won't be able to eject either. Some player software may lock the eject button in hardware, but you can eject using the software eject button on the player.

Assuming the drive is still registered by the BIOS and operating system, you really do have a stuck disc. The next step is to look for a pinhole on the front of the CD or DVD drive. Power down the system and unplug the power cord, then straighten out a couple inches worth of paper clip, the heaviest gauge that will fit in the hole. Gently push the paper clip straight into the hole, until you feel it depress the release mechanism. This will sometime cause the tray to pop out a fraction of an inch, other times you will have to pry it a little to get it started. Once you have enough tray sticking out to grab it with your fingers, you should be able to pull it out. If the faceplate seems to be bulging as you pull, the disc is hung up on it, and the best thing to do is remove the drive from the PC and then remove the faceplate.

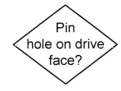

Does the drive cause the whole PC to tremble when it spins up? Is it noisy? Make sure that the drive, if internal, is mounted with four screws, and level. High speed drives will vibrate like crazy if a disc is off balance, usually because the disc itself has some weighting problem. Aside from obvious physical flaws (like the dog or the kid took a bite out of the edge of the disc) a miss-applied label can create an unbalanced disc. Try ejecting and reinserting the disc. I wouldn't keep running a drive that vibrates badly. It could end up damaging the discs (discs have been known to shatter at high speeds) and it doesn't do the other components in your system any good to be vibrated, which can lead to connections working apart or worse. If the problem only occurs with some discs, you can blame the discs. Otherwise, I'd look into a new drive.

Can you listen to music CDs through your speakers? The following assumes that you can get operating system sounds to play from your speakers. If not, proceed to Sound Failure. First, make sure that the CD isn't muted in the software mixer panel. Next, if the drive is equipped with an audio jack on the front, stick in a cheap headphone (if you have one) and see if the CD is playing. In any case, if the CD is spinning and the time is advancing in whatever version of Media Player you have installed, the drive is actually playing the CD. Newer drives support DAE (Digital Audio Extraction) and some SATA drives don't support the old analog audio output at all. If you have a newer drive, check the DAE settings in the drive properties.

Illustrated drive replacement:

www.fonerbooks.com /r_cd.htm

Older drives, both SATA and PATA, required an analog patch cord inside the case. The audio patch cord from the drive to the sound card or the sound port on the motherboard may not be connected, or the device volume could be turned down in a software mixer panel. The easy check for incorrect audio patch cable (3 or 4 wires) connection without opening the PC is to try a multimedia disc, such as a game. Note also that in two drive systems, the builder may only have patched the audio output of one of the drives through to the sound card.

If you can't play movies in your DVD that you can play on a television DVD player, the problem is usually with the software CODEC (Coder/DECoder). Test the movie on a TV first to make sure the disc is good. The media player you are using may display a specific error message, like telling you the screen properties must be set to a certain resolution and number of colors for a movie to play. Or, the player may report that it can't find a decoder (CODEC) to play the particular disc. Even if the movie worked last night, your media player may have received an automated update the next time you went online that rendered the installed CODEC obsolete. If you search the Internet, you'll find plenty of people trying to sell you CODECs, but if you use

Google and stay away from the advertisements, you should be able to get the updated version for free. You may also encounter new copy protection schemes that render some discs unplayable on your PC even though you aren't trying to copy them. The only solution for this again lays in software and Internet research for the specific failure. It may turn out that the only way to render your DVD player compatible with a new type of copy protection is to update the DVD drive firmware. If an update isn't available for your particular model, you can end up out of luck when it comes to playing certain discs from certain studios after a particular date.

Does your problem involve recording CDs or DVDs? If so, proceed to CD/DVD Recording Problems. For a problem booting a factory CD in a recorder, stay here. It's become increasingly difficult to tell factory pressed CDs from recorded CDs, due to the highly polished labels that can be easily printed for recorded CDs and DVDs. Factory produced discs are usually silver on the read surface, while recorded discs are often gold or green.

Does the drive read discs? When you mount a disc, be it software or music, does the drive acknowledge that a disc is present and let you view the contents? It doesn't matter (at this point) whether or not you can get through installing the software on the disc or read all of the information. The question is simply, can the drive see anything at all on the disc?

Does your system refuse to boot known good boot CDs, like operating systems from Windows 98 on up? Try setting the boot sequence in CMOS Setup to boot to the CD or DVD first. This shouldn't really be necessary if the hard drive is uninitiated, but I've seen it fix the problem. I've also seen some high speed drives which take too long to spin up and report to the BIOS that there's a bootable disc present. Sometimes you can get around this by opening and closing the tray, which should cause the drive to spin up, and hitting reset right after you've done so. With any luck, you'll get the timing right so that the BIOS checks for a bootable CD while the drive is still active.

Do you have CD and DVD drives installed? It's easy enough to mix up drives on a PC, and a CD drive isn't going to going to have much luck reading a DVD. A CD recorder along with a DVD player was a common two drive combination years ago, but the DVD may not be able to read CDs recorded just two inches away. See Recording Problems if you're having trouble reading a recorded disc. Some older systems have both a CD ROM (reader) and a CDR (recorder).

Reading right drive?

Are you reading the right drive? If you have two physical drives, make sure the operating system is actually looking at the drive the CD or DVD has been placed in. Trust me, I've been fooled myself into opening up a machine by blind belief in the wrong drive letter. Most drives have an activity LED that tells you when the drive is active. Make sure the activity LED is lighting up on the drive you put the disc in when you try to read it.

Read other discs?

Does the drive read other discs? Try another disc, a factory CD in CD ROMs or CDRs or a factory DVD in DVD ROMs or DVDRs. If it works, the problem is with the media and not the drive. Make sure the disc you can't read is the right type for the drive your are trying it in, ie, CD, DVD, CDR, DVDR, noting that many of the recordable discs won't be readable in other players. Clean the disc with a soft bit of flannel. The discs are plastics, so don't use solvents. Scratches can render a disc unreadable, including scratches on the surface (label), which cause distortions in the layer that is actually being read from the bottom. Try the disc in another reader before chucking it out, it could just have trouble with the device you were trying it in.

Device Manager problem?

Does the drive show up in the operating system, on your desktop or in Device Manager in Windows operating systems? If not, the first step is to reinstall the driver. Get the latest driver from the manufacturer's website and install it. If you can boot an OS CD in the drive, but the drive has disappeared from Device Manager, try reinstalling the OS. Check if there's a firmware update for the drive itself, though flashing a drive, just like flashing a motherboard BIOS, should be a last resort. Even though the BIOS registers the drive's presence, you can still try swapping the ribbon cable. The laser lens in the drive could be incredibly dirty, so if you can find an inexpensive cleaning kit, it's worth a try.

DVD SATA?

If you're using a newer SATA DVD recorder/player, there aren't any jumpers to set or cable sharing issues. If it's a new build, make sure that you don't have the data cable attached to a dedicated SATA RAID controller. But the safest way to determine if there's a problem with your SATA cable, or a compatibility issue with the BIOS, is to try the drive in another PC, or mount it in an external USB shell and connect it externally.

Drive shares IDE cable?

You could have a simple cabling problem or Master/Slave conflict. If the drive is the Slave on primary IDE controller with the hard drive, move it to the secondary IDE controller as the Master (requires another IDE ribbon cable). If you already have another device installed as the secondary Master, try the drive as the secondary Slave or temporarily replace the Master for the sake of seeing if it works.

Recording Problem DVD, CD, Blu Ray

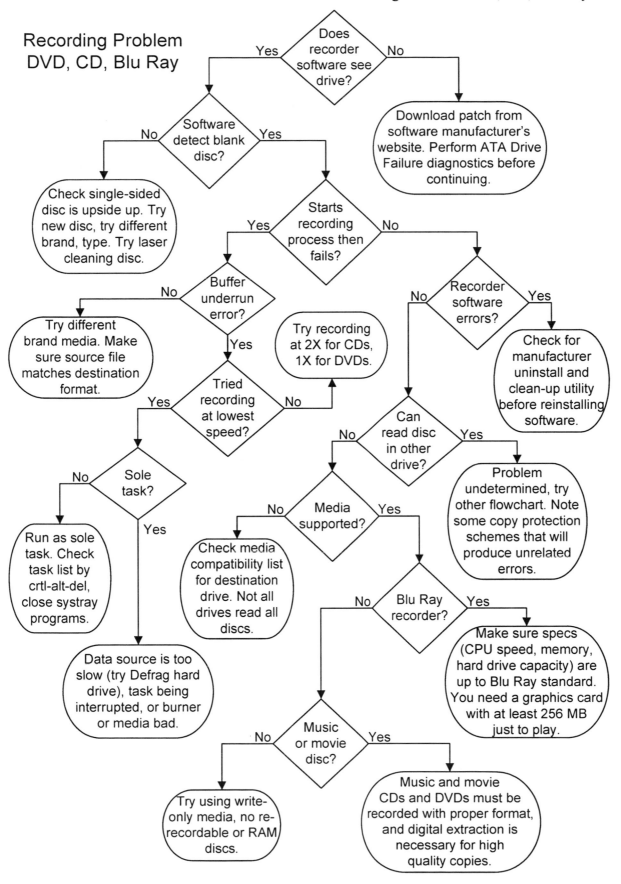

Recording Problem DVD, CD, Blu Ray

Does the recorder software, whether the native operating system software or a third party recording suite, see the burner and correctly identify it? Get the latest version of the driver from the software maker's web site. The fact that the software was packaged with your drive or PC when you bought it doesn't necessarily mean it's up-to-date for your particular model or the operating system release you're running. If your drive was sold with OEM software, rather than a full version, and an update for your drive isn't available, it's possible that software won't work with the drive at all, and you may be stuck buying a retail version. When it comes to software compatibility, start by checking the drive manufacturer's web site. The drive manufacturer may also have a firmware upgrade for the recorder.

Does the recorder software detect that a recordable disc is in the drive? The most common error when using cheap discs sold without any labeling is mounting them in the drive tray upside down. You can try turning the disc over, or if there are numbers printed around the spindle hole in the center of the disc, the disc is upside up when you can read them. Try cleaning the disc. It may be bad, even if it looks perfectly good to the eye (no scratches, fingerprints, etc.) I've seen failure rates as high as 20% or more with cheap discs that have been sitting around for a while. Make sure the disc type you purchased is compatible with your recorder, even if it means trying a more expensive brand the manufacturer recommends. You can try a laser cleaning disc kit from a local office store, but it's a long shot.

Does your recorder begin the recording process, and then fail? Note that this renders the "write only" or "R" as in CDR or DVDR media useless. Some people like using the rewriteable media to test that recording will work before using a write only blank, but so many problems are media specific that I don't really see the point. Failure can be due to anything from bad recording media to failing recorder hardware, but the most common problem is multi-tasking while recording.

If you get a buffer underrun error, it means the recorder has run out of data to write to the disc continually and fails. In today's era of even the slowest hardware being pretty fast, this is usually due to other tasks overtaxing your resources, or a poorly planned recording session. Try defragging the hard drive before you record discs, and if the defrag utility keeps restarting, it's usually a sign that some other task is competing with it for the hard drive's attention. Make sure your virus suite isn't running a full system scan in the background.

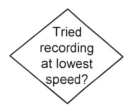

The first thing to check is if the drive successfully records discs to completion at a lower speed (try the lowest speed possible, usually 2X). If your recorder works at lower record speeds, the recordable media you have may not be certified for the higher speed, or it may just not work at the higher speed in your recorder. Brand new certified recording media often turns out to have physical flaws, which kind of defeats the point of it being "certified." Visually inspect the discs you are using and try recording at a higher speed with another brand.

Close all other tasks so that the recording process is the only job your PC is working on. Other tasks can include work you are doing in another program, as well as background tasks, like Internet and fax/phone software. There are various 3rd party software packages capable of controlling background tasks, but you can usually get by with crtl-alt-del and the Windows Task List, once you get a feel for which tasks are superfluous to what you're doing. If the record process won't go through even at 2X, it's possible that all of the media you've tried writing to is either bad or not suited for the recorder you are using. It's also possible that the recorder is kaput. After you eliminate media as a problem, try moving the recorder to another machine and installing all of the latest software (both drivers and burner software) before giving up on it.

Does your recording software generate errors with cryptic code numbers? Recording software goes through frequent updates and requires high level access to the PC's resources. Previously installed recorder programs or even previous versions of the same software can cause errors in the management of the recording session. Check the software maker's website for a specific uninstall and clean-up utility before reinstalling the latest version.

Does the disc record properly, read or play fine in the drive you recorded it in, but fail to play in other computer drives or in consumer devices, such as stereos and DVD players? The rewriteable media often fails completely in read-only drives, like standard CD ROM drives or DVD set-top boxes. Check with the manufacturer of the target device, the device you want to read the recorded disc in, to make sure you are using a compatible media and format. There are a sickening number of official formats and variations for recordable CDs and DVDs and many of them aren't supported by commercial playback devices, and never will be. The rule of thumb for recording data CDs that will be readable in the majority of CD drives is to use the write-once, CDR media.

Does the device you are trying to play the newly recorded disc in support that media and format? A movie or audio disc that plays fine in your recorder thanks to the proper laser wavelength or the installed CODECs will not necessarily be readable in other computer drives or consumer devices. Check the specifications for the player you are targeting on the Internet, for both the specific format you are recording and the type of recordable media. If the media or format you are using isn't explicitly compatible, there's a good chance it won't work.

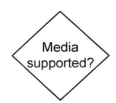

Blu Ray recorders have extended the capacity of standard DVDs by a factor of five, from 4.7 GB for a single sided single layered DVD, to 25 GB for a single sided single layer Blu Ray disc. But with all that capacity comes the requirement for computer hardware fast enough to read and process the stream of data. PC owners have long been used to being able to buy any peripherals sold in the store and assume that they will work with their systems as long as the operating system is up to date. But Blu Ray drives require a fairly high performance CPU, and plenty of RAM and hard drive space. They also require a video card with 256 MB RAM, just for playing back high resolution movies. While most gaming PCs built in the last few years will meet the requirements, the average consumer or business PC will not.

For high quality copying of music or video, digital extraction is the only way to go. Digital Audio Extraction (DAE) has long been available on most optical PC drives. On older DVD and CD drives, you need a hard wired connection between the DAE out from the drive and the sound card or motherboard. On newer DVD or Blu Ray drives, the DAE function should work over the SATA data cable, but check your drive to be sure.

There are too many available formats for audio and video to get into in a troubleshooting book, but the basic concept remains, garbage in, garbage out. You aren't going to get a copy that's better than the original source, so recording an early, low resolution MPEG file onto a Blu Ray disc isn't going to improve the playback, and the recording software may refuse to even work with the older formats. Most of the file formats are easily investigated by searching online, Wikipedia has some excellent write-ups. The only acronym you might trip over without recognizing is VCD (Video Compact Disc) which used the MPEG-1 CODEC to create video discs in older CD recorders. Note that many of the intermediate solutions for increasing capacity involved non-standard discs and recording practices, and these discs are rarely portable to a wide variety of playback devices.

Music CDs that you want to play in a stereo must be recorded on CDR, not CDRW, and the burner software must be set to record them in the CD-DA (Redbook) format. Writing a bunch of .wav files to a CD, even at the proper sampling frequency and in stereo, will not result in a CD that's playable in a stereo. It's the format that counts. You don't have to buy the more expensive CDR blanks labeled "CD Audio" blanks or the like, these are only required for dedicated (non PC connected) CDR devices. DVD players usually support multiple media types, but you need to check the documentation for the final word.

Finally, some manufactured discs are created with copy protection that can have unexpected results if you attempt to make copies. The copying process may go through without a hitch but leave you with a copy that doesn't play, or the software might report various errors. And some studio movie discs will not play in PCs if they employ protection that isn't incorporated into the latest version of the operating system media player.

Modem Failure

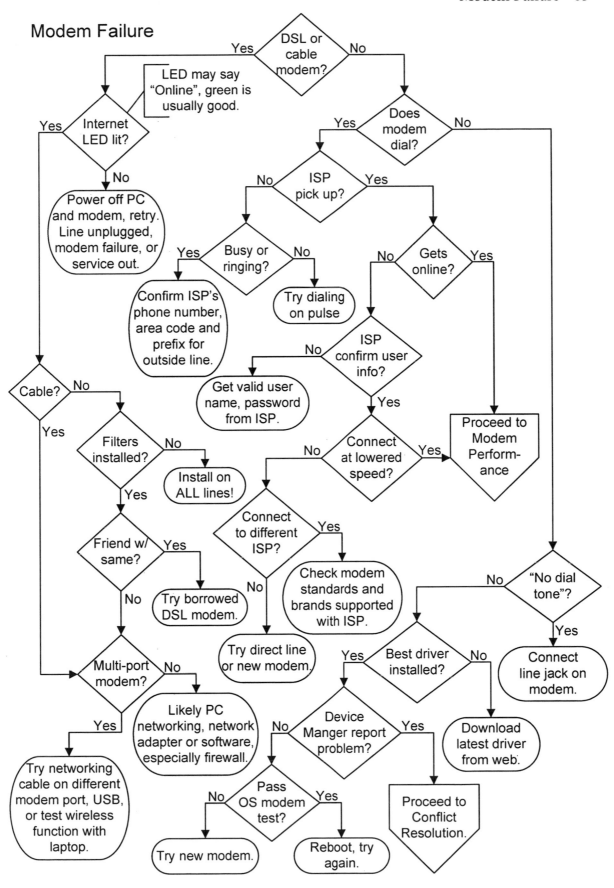

Modem Failure

Do you have a high speed Internet connection using the phone line for DSL (Digital Subscriber Line) or through the cable TV network? The vast majority of high speed connections are accomplished through an external modem or modem/router, which provides for both the high speed connection to the Internet and supports connections to multiple PCs. Newer DSL modems almost always include a wireless router to support laptops, the cable companies are running a little behind, so a separate wireless router may be required.

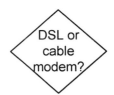

Does your modem actually dial the phone? If you have a desktop PC, there should be a little piezoelectric speaker on the modem itself. Many people (and computer vendors) turn down the volume for this in software, which you can find on the "Properties" tab of the modems in Windows Control Panel. Notebook computers will normally run the sound through the notebook speakers, which means the volume controls in Windows and the volume dial built into the notebook body must both be turned up.

Does the ISP answer? You should be able to hear the ISP's modem pick up and whistle and hiss back at your modem through the speaker. If not, make sure you are dialing the right phone number and that the ISP isn't temporarily down. Just dial the number from a regular phone handset and the ISP modem should pick up and whistle at you.

Make sure you have the area code and any prefix for an outside line correct, especially if you are dialing from a business. Dial-up lines in a business must have a clean path through a business phone system (PBX - Private Branch eXchange), just like fax lines. If the phone is always busy, call the ISP's tech support or try one of the other phone numbers they provide. It could simply be that they don't have enough modems available for the traffic in your area at certain times of day.

If you hear the modem dial but the dial tone remains until an operator picks up and tells you that your phone is off hook, you're trying to use "tone" dialing on a "pulse" system. This is easily changed in the "Dialing Properties" of the basic modem page in Control Panel.

Do you get an error stating that the ISP can't negotiate a connection, protocol, anything along those lines? Unfortunately, this error is too generic to help much with troubleshooting. Even messages telling you to check your password can be caused by just about anything. Try redialing several times without changing anything to make sure you aren't just encountering an overloaded modem pool.

Illustrated modem
replacement:

www.fonerbooks.com
/r_modem.htm

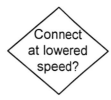

Call your ISP on the phone to confirm your login information if it's the first time you're dialing in. Re-enter your password, remembering that caps usually count. Assuming you have your username and password right, the odds are any errors reported aren't due to any protocol settings on your part, especially if you haven't changed the defaults. If the error crops up at random, it's usually due to the weather and the time of day, as both play a major role in the circuit conditions of the telco infrastructure. Stormy or damp weather can badly degrade the lines of older telephone networks. The time of day is also important, with the beginning of the business day, and a period in the mid-afternoon usually being the worst times. I've actually run non-Internet modem applications on dedicated lines that showed a huge increase of line noise during these periods, whatever your telco tells you.

Will your modem connect at a lower speed? You can change the maximum speed the modem will try to connect at in Control Panel, but I've noted that the settings don't always take effect, even after rebooting. You can search on the Internet for the modem control string to force your modem to V.34 compatibility, then insert it in the Advanced Settings for the modem which can be accessed through the Modem Properties in Control Panel or Device Manager. If you succeed in connecting at a lower speed, try going through the Modem Performance diagnostics.

Can you connect to a different ISP? The best test for eliminating modem failure is to see if it will connect to a different service. If you can connect to a friend's ISP, it's a definite proof that the modem isn't bad. It doesn't mean that the ISP you can't connect to is at fault, it could be a question of matching modem standards. By the same token, if you can't connect to another ISP, it doesn't prove your modem is faulty, it could still be a problem with line conditions.

If the software reports, "No Dial Tone", make sure you have the patch cord from the modem to the wall jack plugged into the "line" jack of the modem. The "phone" jack on the modem is for plugging in a regular telephone to use when you aren't online. If the wall jack is live, try changing the telephone patch cord running from the "line" jack on the modem to the jack on the wall. Check the phone jack at the wall with a telephone handset. If it doesn't work you need to repair the in-wall wiring or try a different jack.

Have you installed the most recent driver you can find on the modem manufacturer's web site? If your modem is integrated on the motherboard, it would be an update to your motherboard driver. Even if your modem is brand-new, hardware often ships with obsolete drivers, either because it's been sitting on the shelf somewhere for a year, or because a recent operating system release has overtaken it and a better driver is available.

Does the operating system report the modem as present and operating? This information appears in Device Manager in Windows. If not, reinstall the driver for the modem. If an IRQ conflict is reported in Device Manager, resolve it by either changing IRQ in software (with a plug-n-play modem) or changing the IRQ jumper on the modem for an old card. If you absolutely can't get around it, you may have an extremely unfriendly sound card or other adapter on the bus which is hogging the IRQ the modem is capable of dealing with. Note that a modem can share an IRQ with a serial port in some cases, though it can't be used when a device is actually attached to that port. If you can't resolve the Device Manager problem, either you have a hardware conflict, or the modem is bad. Proceed to the Conflict Resolution chart.

Does the operating system or dialing software report the port is "in use" when you try to dial? In Windows Control Panel > Modems, go to "Diagnostics," select your modem, and click on "More Info". Try shutting down and rebooting. The "port in use" error is due to another active software application claiming the port the modem is set on. You could get this error if you're already using the modem but don't realize it for some reason, but it's more likely that you've recently installed software for synchronizing a palm device or for a camera that's colliding with the modem driver.

High speed modems, whether DSL or cable, come equipped with a number of status LEDs that report on the condition of the modem. The LED we are interested in here is the one that reports on the status of the Internet connection to the modem. When the modem is powered on, this is the last LED to display a steady state status. Most DSL modems and some cable modems also feature an LED that simply reports whether or not the modem sees a live connection to the cable company or to the phone company. When the Internet LED is off or red, make sure the cable or DSL line is connected, turn off the modem and the PC and try restarting just the modem, giving it a few minutes to negotiate the connection. The problem might be that service in your area is out, but check the obvious before calling the provider.

Do you have a cable modem? Cable modems are somewhat simpler to troubleshoot, so the flowchart skips a few steps here that aren't applicable to cable modems. One of the steps we skip is simply swapping your modem with that of a friend or neighbor. While it might work in some cases, cable companies are far more finicky about installed hardware than phone companies due to their fear of people pirating cable signals, so it's not a positive test. If you are having drop-out problems with a cable modem, it makes sense to simplify the modem's connection to the cable interface in your home, especially if you are using and coaxial switch boxes.

DSL modems are shipped from the Internet provider with a number of filters that you are supposed to install on every other phone connection on the circuit that's in use. Not installing the filters leads to two problems. First, you'll hear constant static on the regular phones when you try to talk, which should be enough of a reason to install them. But some digital phone devices, such as answering machines or faxes, may also interfere with the DSL modem's ability to negotiate an Internet connection unless the filters are installed. Consult the instructions that come with the filters if you aren't sure where to use them. If you are setting up a DSL modem for the first time and can't get an Internet connection (assuming the phone company assures you it's live), you can also try unplugging any other phone devices in the house to make sure they aren't causing a problem.

One easy way to test if your DSL modem has failed on most systems is to borrow the identical working DSL modem from a friend or neighbor using the same system. Likewise, if your friends are brave, you can try installing your DSL modem on their line and seeing if it works, which eliminates the possibility that the modem is good and your incoming phone line has problems.

If your modem only supports a single networking connection and USB, but you can't get online with your PC, try changing to the other connection and reinstalling the software supplied by the service provider. Replace the networking or USB cable with a known good cable. If you have a true modem/router, try connecting the networking cable from your PC to a different port, even if the status LED indicated the other port connection was good. If the router supports wireless, borrow a laptop and see if you can get online, and then turn off wireless and connect the laptop directly to eliminate the possibility that you have a failed network adapter or bad USB port in the PC.

If the hardware all tests good through the laptop or through your taking it to a friend's to test, but your PC network adapter or USB port are also working, the problem is software settings. Uninstall the software from the Internet provider and then try reinstalling, making sure you follow their instructions to the letter about the sequence of steps. Make sure your virus suite and firewall software aren't blocking Internet access and contact the tech support for your Internet provider who can walk you through all of the settings in Windows.

Modem Performance

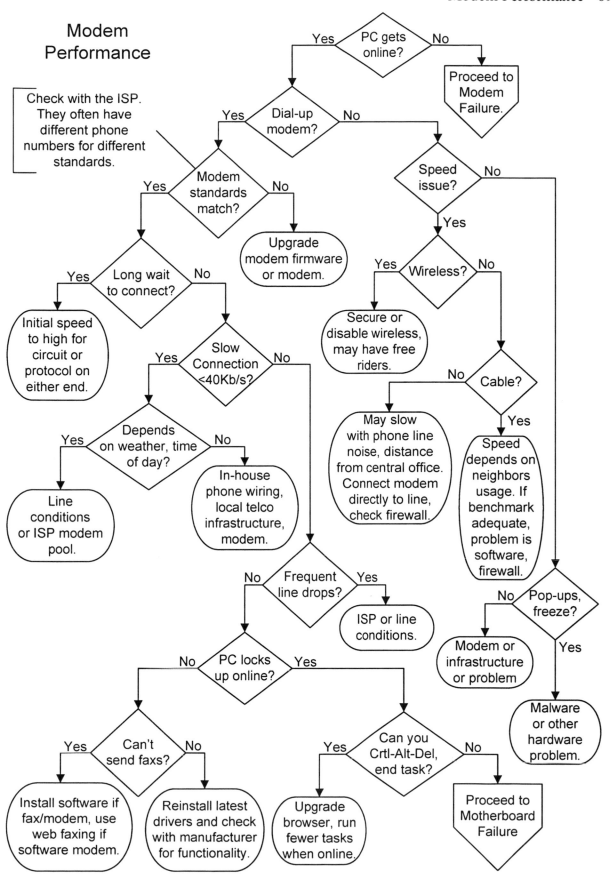

Check with the ISP. They often have different phone numbers for different standards.

PC gets online?
- Yes →
- No → Proceed to Modem Failure.

Dial-up modem?
- Yes →
- No → Speed issue?

Modem standards match?
- Yes →
- No → Upgrade modem firmware or modem.

Long wait to connect?
- Yes → Initial speed to high for circuit or protocol on either end.
- No → Slow Connection <40Kb/s?

Slow Connection <40Kb/s?
- Yes → Depends on weather, time of day?
- No → Frequent line drops?

Depends on weather, time of day?
- Yes → Line conditions or ISP modem pool.
- No → In-house phone wiring, local telco infrastructure, modem.

Speed issue?
- No →
- Yes → Wireless?

Wireless?
- Yes → Secure or disable wireless, may have free riders.
- No → Cable?

Cable?
- No → May slow with phone line noise, distance from central office. Connect modem directly to line, check firewall.
- Yes → Speed depends on neighbors usage. If benchmark adequate, problem is software, firewall.

Frequent line drops?
- No → PC locks up online?
- Yes → ISP or line conditions.

PC locks up online?
- No → Can't send faxs?
- Yes → Can you Crtl-Alt-Del, end task?

Can't send faxs?
- Yes → Install software if fax/modem, use web faxing if software modem.
- No → Reinstall latest drivers and check with manufacturer for functionality.

Can you Crtl-Alt-Del, end task?
- Yes → Upgrade browser, run fewer tasks when online.
- No → Proceed to Motherboard Failure

Pop-ups, freeze?
- No → Modem or infrastructure or problem
- Yes → Malware or other hardware problem.

Modem Performance

Can you access the Internet through your PC and modem combination? We're talking about getting online, being able to run a Google search or access your e-mail. If not, see the modem failure flowchart.

Old fashioned dial-up modems actually have far more performance related problems than newer high speed modems connected to the phone company by DSL or to the cable provider via a cable modem. The one thing they all have in common is that if your PC has been taken over by malware, it will run slow no matter how you connect.

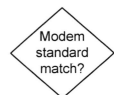

Does your modem standard match one of the modem standards supported by the ISP? The most recent standard for 56K dial-up modems is V.92, though the majority of ISPs are probably still on V.90. The two previous 56K standards still widely supported by ISPs are k56Flex and X2. The previous 33K standards, V.32 and V.34 are probably more universally supported than the early 56K standards. Many of the 33K pre-V.90 modems can actually be upgraded to V.90 through a flash upgrade of the adapter BIOS, obtained through the manufacturer.

Almost all modems sold in the last ten years will support V.90 or V.92, but some rural ISP's have yet to implement it and are still running one of the original 56K standards, k56Flex or X2. Often times, local ISPs don't really know what they are doing and will blame any problems on your modem, until you buy one that happens to match their network. If your ISP claims to support all of these but "suggests" you try V.90, I'd take that to mean that their support is conditional, and you're better off getting a V.90 or V.92 modem if you want to connect to them with any success. Before you replace a modem, you should really try it with another ISP. If it works fine with them, you can make an informed decision as to whether you want to play musical modems until you get one that your current ISP is compatible with, or jump ship.

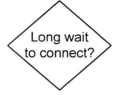

Does it take your modem up to a half a minute or longer to obtain a connection after the answering modem picks up? There are several possibilities, but the most likely is that your modem is capable of a much higher connection speed than the circuit, for various reasons, can support. The endless negotiation between your modem and the ISP modem can be a result of slowly ratcheting down the speed on both ends until a satisfactory error rate is reached. This could be due to a failing modem, but it's more often infrastructure or line conditions that limit connection speed.

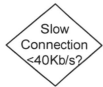

Is your connection speed always much lower than the modem rating? Most people have 56K modems that should get connections ranging from 40K to 53K in ideal conditions. It could be that your modem speed is actually set too low in software, or that you are using some error checking or compression algorithm that isn't ideal for the circuit. Make a note of all of your current settings before you start making changes, and note that in some cases, you'll have to reboot before they take effect. Make sure you check the Extra Settings field in the modem connection Advanced Properties menu. It could also be that your phone wiring simply isn't going to support a higher speed, that you are too far from the central office, or they just haven't upgraded their infrastructure to support digital signaling, in which case you'll never get a connection over 33K. Your ISP may not really support higher speeds, or they may have a mix of modem banks such that your connection speed appears to be random.

If your connection speed depends on the weather or the time of day, it's probably due to line conditions. The worst times to dial into the web are usually at the start of the business day and when school lets out. This is due to the noise on the copper phone lines generated by the heavy use at these times. The weather effect depends on the quality of your telephone company infrastructure. I have firsthand experience with poor local infrastructure murdering connection speed. My old notebook computer rarely got connections over 33K and suffered frequent line-drops when dialing into a local ISP. When I took the notebook on a trip to Florida, 1100 miles away, and dialed into the same ISP phone number by long distance, I got stable 52K connections every time. The area of Florida I was visiting had new phone infrastructure using lots of fiber optics, as opposed to the 80 year old copper in my New England town!

Do you suffer from frequent disconnects? The first thing to check if you have line drops is whether you have call waiting and a modem/ISP that doesn't support call waiting. If you don't have call waiting, line drops are usually a result of the ISP being over burdened, or really bad line conditions. The ISP will rarely admit that their system is dropping lines, so it's a tough one to diagnose with 100% certainty. There's nothing you can do about the telco infrastructure, but you can get the cleanest connection possible in your house by reducing the number of connections between your PC and the incoming phone line. You can also try running your modem at a lower speed. In extreme cases, you can try replacing your modem, but I'd probably try a new ISP first. You may determine that the problem is with the infrastructure of the telephone company or some other external factors, such as the wiring in your part of town being routed alongside an incredibly noisy electrical transformer, etc. There's nothing you can do about the weather, but you can work around the time of day problem by identifying the good times to call in and sticking with them.

Does the whole computer sometimes lock up when you're online, forcing you to shut down and reboot? If it always happens at the same web site, it's probably an incompatibility with the web browser version and software plug-ins. You may need to enable Java Script or download and install a browser upgrade to access certain sites. The important thing to understand is if the lock-up only occurs on certain sites, it's not a modem issue.

If you can get a live task list with crt-alt-del, shut down the browser and continue, it's probably a software conflict or an incompatible web application. Browsers sometimes lock up if you try to access your favorites list before the browser has finished loading. You could also be suffering lock-ups due to lack of RAM or CPU overheating problems, so start again at the Motherboard, CPU and RAM Failure diagnostics.

Do you want to send or receive faxes but you can't figure out how? The first thing to check is whether or not you have a fax/modem. If it wasn't sold as a fax/modem and the driver doesn't identify it as a fax modem, it's not a fax and you can't directly use it to send and receive faxes. You can still use a web based fax service. If you do have a fax/modem and can't fax, it's just a question of installing (or finding) the proper software, which should have come on CD with the fax/modem.

Does it seem like your high speed connection isn't that fast? Malware and viruses can kill your performance, but so can aggressive firewall settings, which is why most firewall software includes a lower security setting for when you are running online games which require maximum interactivity and performance. In order to test your physical connection speed before you complain to your Internet provider, check their website for a speed testing tool, or try a third party speed checker. I'd recommend Googling "Bandwidth Meter" and using the CNET speed tester, assuming they keep it online.

Does your modem/router support a wireless connection? If it does, have you established a secure password for accessing the Internet? If you live in an urban area and you haven't secured your modem, it's almost a given that neighbors will be borrowing some of your bandwidth with their laptops, often unintentionally because they simply connect to the network that works. If there's a wireless LED on your modem/router and it's going nuts when you aren't using a laptop yourself, create a wireless password or disable the wireless function.

Are you running a cable modem? Unlike DSL modems which are directly connected to the phone company central office by your phone line, cable modems are pooled together in such a way that they share the available bandwidth. If your speed varies widely throughout the day, there's nothing wrong with your connection, it's just a question of usage patterns. If you have some neighbors who spend all their waking hours downloading movies from the Internet, you just aren't going to see the maximum cable performance. As with all modems, it's also a good idea to make your cable connection as clean as possible, eliminating extra switches and splitters between the modem and the incoming line.

DSL modems must be within a few miles of the phone switching office to work, and as you get near the limits, the performance may drop off due to higher error rates. You might also see performance degradation with weather conditions or during high phone use periods during the business day. Check again that you are using filters on all phone extensions with devices (phones, answering machines, etc) connected. If benchmarking software shows you aren't getting the speed you are paying for, your only choice may be cable.

Both cable and DSL connected PCs will see a huge knock on performance if they have been taken over by malware. If you aren't running a virus protection suite including anti-virus, anti-adware and a firewall, you should install one. If your PC behaves strangely, if your home page has changed to some generic looking directory site you've never heard of or if you get endless pop-ups trying to sell you things, your PC has been infected or hijacked by malware. However, if your PC frequently freezes up or generates cryptic messages about memory errors, it's more likely that you have a hardware problem, and should refer to the flowchart for motherboard, CPU and RAM performance first.

If your Internet connection works fast when it's working, but frequently disconnects or glitches, it's likely a modem problem or a problem with service provider. Don't be afraid to call tech support to complain, but first start a log of when and in what circumstances the problems occur. Not only will that help convince the service provider that you're serious, it may help you diagnose the problem before you have to spend an hour trying to get through to a human being. Cable modem wiring within the house tends to be simpler than DSL wiring, since you have a limited number of cable devices. If you are using multiple telephone line splitters in the connection to your DSL modem, it could be something as silly as a poor connection in one of them that gets shaken up when you use a particular phone extension. Always connect your DSL modem directly into a telephone wall jack.

Sound
Failure

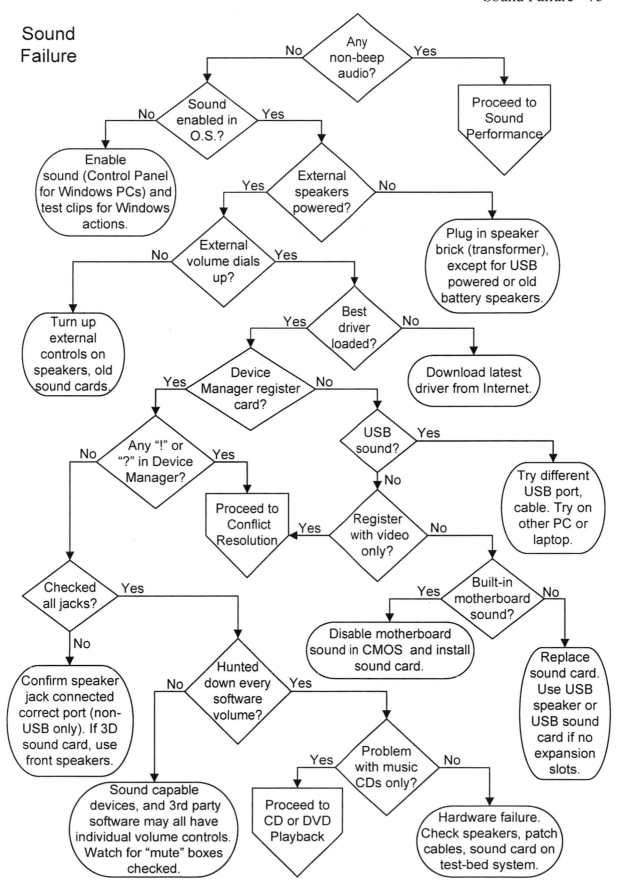

Sound Failure

Do you get any audio out of the PC other than beeps on power-up? The beeps you hear on power-up are not part of the PC's sound system, they are generated by a tiny piezoelectric speaker on the motherboard that is included strictly for diagnostic codes. If you are getting any other audio from the PC, music, chimes, etc, the sound hardware hasn't failed, so you can proceed to the sound performance flowchart.

Is sound enabled in the operating system? In Windows, the basic "Sounds" menu is found in Control Panel. Sound events that have little speakers next to them are enabled. Enable sounds for some actions that you recognize (like "exit program" or "minimize") and see if your speakers work now. Note that operating system sounds don't need to be enabled for music CDs or games to work, but if you're here, we're starting off with the assumption that you aren't getting any sound out of the speakers at all.

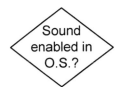

Are the speakers plugged in to a power source? The volume control on speakers usually serves as an on/off as well. There are some super cheap speakers that don't offer amplification, in which case there won't be any power cord, but don't expect much in terms of volume or quality. Really ancient speakers may be powered by batteries rather than a transformer, so if your speakers don't have a power cord, double check that they don't have a hatch for batteries.

The oldest sound cards have a manual volume dial, as do most external speakers. Manual volume dials should be adjusted to somewhere in the middle of the range, not all the way to one extreme or the other. Did you check? Check again. You don't want to invite a friend over to help with your sound problem, only to find the volume is manually turned down.

Have you loaded the best driver for the sound card? The best driver means the most recent driver, so check the manufacturer's website for an update, because your sound card may have been sitting on a shelf for a year before you bought it. If the sound is integrated on the motherboard, check for an update at your motherboard manufacturer's web site.

Does Device Manager register the sound card or integrated motherboard audio and report that the device is working properly? Even if you don't have the proper driver, Device Manager will probably identify it as a sound controller. Before you start stripping

down the system or chase off to conflict resolution, make sure the adapter is seated in the motherboard slot.

If the Device Manager reports a resource conflict between any of the audio devices and another device, look through all of your device reports and figure out where the conflict is. It may be resolvable by changing the settings in Device Manager, or it may take aggressive reshuffling of adapters. If you get a "!," "?" or "i" on the sound controller in Device Manager, proceed to Conflict Resolution.

Check your documentation or the symbols on the sound card to make sure you actually have the speakers plugged into the proper jack. On high-end sound cards with front and rear speaker jacks, try the front speaker jack first. Check that your audio patch cables are all plugged firmly into the proper jacks and that the cables aren't damaged. If you have USB speakers, they don't jack directly into the sound card.

Software volume controls are the #1 problem with sound, and a real pain to figure out if multiple people use the system. Aside from the primary volume control often found in your system tray, there are various other mixer panels and volume adjustments that get installed with the driver and are offered in various applications. All of these can cause a complete absence of sound if the "mute" box is checked. I don't have any magic method for finding the mixer panel or any additional volume controls in a typical system. The Multimedia icon in Control Panel is a good place to start.

Does your sound system work properly with everything except music CDs? If so, proceed to CD and DVD Playback diagnostics. One good test is to try the speakers and cables on another system, or another device with a speaker jack, like a portable radio. Make sure you first turn the speaker volume control all the way down in case the output is already amplified. If your speakers and cables don't work anywhere, try swapping the cables to find out which is faulty. If the speakers and cables are good, either the sound card is blown or you didn't look hard enough for a hidden mute in software.

If you are using USB speakers or a full USB sound card, try connecting them to a different USB port. USB ports often break inside the PC when the cords are jerked or tripped over. If you can't get the USB sound device to function on the PC, test it on any other PC or laptop. If it works on another computer, you know that the problem is either that all of your USB ports have failed, which would usually mean the USB controller on the motherboard popped, that the driver software is incompatible, or that you didn't find a "mute" in the OS.

If Device Manager only registers the sound card when you strip out all the adapters except the video card, it's definitely a conflict. If it's a new build or a new sound card, make sure you followed the installation instructions, which may have specified that you must install the software before installing the hardware. If that was the case and you did it backwards, remove the sound card, uninstall the software through Windows Control Panel > Add/Remove Programs, and start over. If you have another sound card lying around, it's a good time to try it; otherwise proceed to Conflict Resolution.

If your only audio support is built into the motherboard, make sure it's enabled in CMOS Setup. If you are using a sound card, make sure any motherboard audio is disabled in CMOS Setup. The easiest way to replace a motherboard integrated sound card is to pick up USB speakers (the sound card is built into the speakers) or a full USB sound hub. The only potential problem with these is if you have an older CD or DVD drive that doesn't support DAE (Digital Audio Extraction). Without DAE, USB sound devices won't be able to play music CDs.

If you can't get the operating system to recognize an installed sound card, which is sure to be plug-and-play, shut down and unplug, remove all the other adapters except the video card from the system, reboot and let the BIOS and operating system adjust. Then shut down and unplug again, add the sound card, and see if you can get it going. If this works, you might still have problems when you add the other adapters back in, but if you do it one at a time, at least you'll find out for sure where the conflict lies.

Illustrated sound card replacement

www.fonerbooks.com /r_sound.htm

Sound and Game Controller Performance

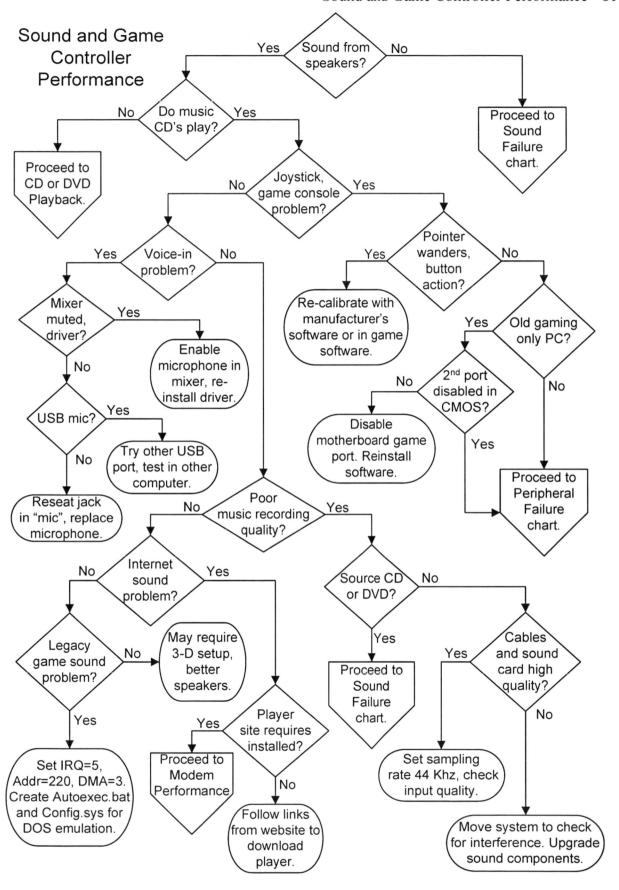

- **Sound from speakers?** — Yes → Do music CD's play? / No → Proceed to Sound Failure chart.
- **Proceed to Sound Failure chart.**
- **Do music CD's play?** — No → Proceed to CD or DVD Playback. / Yes → Joystick, game console problem?
- **Proceed to CD or DVD Playback.**
- **Joystick, game console problem?** — No → Voice-in problem? / Yes → Pointer wanders, button action?
- **Pointer wanders, button action?** — Yes → Re-calibrate with manufacturer's software or in game software. / No → Old gaming only PC?
- **Re-calibrate with manufacturer's software or in game software.**
- **Old gaming only PC?** — Yes → 2nd port disabled in CMOS? / No → Proceed to Peripheral Failure chart.
- **2nd port disabled in CMOS?** — No → Disable motherboard game port. Reinstall software. / Yes → Proceed to Peripheral Failure chart.
- **Disable motherboard game port. Reinstall software.**
- **Proceed to Peripheral Failure chart.**
- **Voice-in problem?** — Yes → Mixer muted, driver? / No → Poor music recording quality?
- **Mixer muted, driver?** — Yes → Enable microphone in mixer, re-install driver. / No → USB mic?
- **Enable microphone in mixer, re-install driver.**
- **USB mic?** — Yes → Try other USB port, test in other computer. / No → Reseat jack in "mic", replace microphone.
- **Try other USB port, test in other computer.**
- **Reseat jack in "mic", replace microphone.**
- **Poor music recording quality?** — No → Internet sound problem? / Yes → Source CD or DVD?
- **Internet sound problem?** — No → Legacy game sound problem? / Yes → May require 3-D setup, better speakers.
- **Legacy game sound problem?** — No → May require 3-D setup, better speakers. / Yes → Set IRQ=5, Addr=220, DMA=3. Create Autoexec.bat and Config.sys for DOS emulation.
- **May require 3-D setup, better speakers.**
- **Set IRQ=5, Addr=220, DMA=3. Create Autoexec.bat and Config.sys for DOS emulation.**
- **Player site requires installed?** — Yes → Proceed to Modem Performance / No → Follow links from website to download player.
- **Proceed to Modem Performance**
- **Follow links from website to download player.**
- **Source CD or DVD?** — Yes → Proceed to Sound Failure chart. / No → Cables and sound card high quality?
- **Proceed to Sound Failure chart.**
- **Cables and sound card high quality?** — Yes → Set sampling rate 44 Khz, check input quality. / No → Move system to check for interference. Upgrade sound components.
- **Set sampling rate 44 Khz, check input quality.**
- **Move system to check for interference. Upgrade sound components.**

Sound and Game Controller Performance

Do you get any sound out of the speakers when the computer boots? If not, unless you've intentionally turned off the operating system sounds, proceed to Sound Failure diagnostics.

Can you hear a music CD through the speakers when the operating system shows that one is being played? Note, if you can't even get the Media Player software to report that it's playing the CD, you either have a Media Player or drive problem rather than an audio problem. Unless you have USB speakers, proceed to the CD or DVD Performance chart. If you do have USB speakers, your CD player and your sound card or motherboard must support Digital Audio Extraction (DAE) for the digital stream to be fed to the speakers. The DAE output on older CD or DVD drives must be hooked to the proper port on the sound card or motherboard as well.

Do you have a problem with the operation of your joystick, game console, other gaming input device? This includes both USB and game port devices. The first trick is to reboot and see if the problem goes away, and the second is to reinstall the software that came with the device. Also make sure that the gaming device is explicitly supported by the game you are using for best performance and the ability to tweak the settings.

Does the joystick pointer wander when you aren't moving your hand, or plough off in some direction by itself? Are you getting unexpected results from the buttons on the joystick? Either the application software (game) or the joystick software should support a calibration procedure for curing drift, assigning buttons, etc. However, older games with limited Windows or DirectX support may simply not work with USB devices, or even game port joysticks that don't resemble the original joysticks. Try using the "Game Controllers" tab in Windows Control Panel to configure and test the device.

If you've kept a ten year old PC around to play games that don't work under new operating systems, you may be using the old fashioned game ports that were present on sound cards and some motherboards. There may be multiple 15 pin game ports installed in an old system. If you have multiple game ports, try your joystick on the other game port. Try reinstalling the device driver, ensuring Device Manager registers the game ports or device. The joystick or game device could actually be bad, so test it on another system. If the joystick works with some other game, the problem is actually with the compatibility of the joystick with the particular game software.

If you have both a game port equipped sound card and a gameport integrated on the motherboard, try disabling the motherboard port in CMOS Setup. Reinstall the device driver for the sound card and run the joystick on the soundcard game port. On PCs old enough to have multiple game ports on the sound card or motherboard, you may have to use jumpers to disable the port.

Is your problem with voice recording or speech recognition? Check that you have the mic in the proper port. If you are doing speech recognition, you should purchase a quality noise cancellation mic, and go through the calibration and testing procedures your software will support. Make sure that the audio driver for the mic is set to the maximum quality (try Multimedia Devices in Control Panel). If you still have a sound quality problem, you may need to replace your sound card, or disable motherboard audio and install a sound card.

Make sure that the microphone isn't muted in the software mixer panel. Check Device Manager for any problems, and if there are any warnings ("!", "?", "i") next to the sound card, reinstall the driver. If reinstalling the driver doesn't clear up the warning, proceed to Conflict Resolution. If the mute box is unchecked and there isn't a driver problem, double check that the microphone jack is in the "mic" port and if it still fails, try the microphone on another audio device and replace it if it's bad.

First, try the mic on a different USB port. A USB microphone also serves as a sound card, since its communication with the PC is strictly digital. That means that the PC's sound card isn't involved at all with the troubleshooting, and you can easily test whether or not the USB mic is working properly by trying it on any other PC or laptop. If the USB mic is good but it doesn't work properly on your PC, there's a problem with your USB ports, the overall performance of the PC being too slow, or with the particular recording software you are using.

Does the music you record sound poor when you play it back? Check your patch cables and jacks for loose connections. Some cables are extremely low quality, so if you plan to do a lot of audio work, start by getting a good set. Make sure that your mixer settings (the software mixer panel) aren't uneven, muting the channels you want, or simply running an unexpected mix. Try muting any inactive channels, which may be introducing white noise. Don't neglect to check the quality of the audio source - if you're trying to record from a hissing tape or a scratchy recording, the sound card does not automatically filter out the unwanted noise. High end recording software does give you the option to clean up recordings, but usually after the recording process is complete.

The quality of any sound recorder is limited by the quality of the source. If you are recording from a CD or DVD, you should be using Digital Audio Extraction (DAE) to make a copy of the audio source files, not playing back through a sound card. If you try recording from MPEG or other compressed files by playing back into a mic or line-in, the quality can only get worse.

First, check the sampling rate is set to 44 Khz (audio CD quality) or higher. Interference is always a possibility, especially if it takes the form of loud ticking. Try moving the system to another location if you're recording near any electrical motors or other possible sources of low frequency interference. True audiophiles spend hundreds of dollars (or more) on audio patch cables that could be worn as jewellery, given the rare metals the wiring is drawn from. They also spend hundreds of dollars on sound cards, and although these are marketed for their playback rather than recording quality, you get what you pay for.

Is your problem related to playing Internet radio or other web based audio applications? If the quality stinks, it's probably your connection to the Internet. If you have a broadband (cable, DSL) connection and the quality still stinks, it could be that your PC is under-powered, you're running too many tasks at the same time or the hard drive is near full and virtual memory is thrashing it.

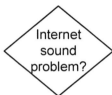

Some Internet audio applications use a third party player, such as Real Audio. If you get no Internet sound at all, but all other audio applications work, your OS and the player software aren't getting along. All you can do is try reinstalling the latest edition. There's usually a link to a site from which you can download a free copy of the player, though it can take a while and you may have to reboot when it's done.

There are a number of reasons the sound quality on your system may not match your experience on somebody else's machine. You may have previously played a game on a better system than yours, one that supported 3D (basically quadraphonics with processing thrown in) sound. The sound card or motherboard audio in your system may be lower quality. The same for the speakers. You could also be picking up interference on the speaker wires, so try routing them away from the computer (and especially keep them away from the monitor).

Is the audio problem with an older game? Rather than try to differentiate between older and newer games, this question could be, "Does sound work properly with any game?" Older games mainly require obsolete sound card compatibility. The default settings of IRQ=5, Address=220, DMA=5 are usually required, since the game communicated directly with the sound card. You may be able to force your sound card to these settings, or, when supported by the driver, you might get by with emulating them under the sound card setup in Device Manager. There's also the possibility, if your game actually exits and runs in DOS mode, that you need to have the proper drivers installed in the DOS Startup files, config.sys and autoexec.bat.

Network Hardware Diagnostics

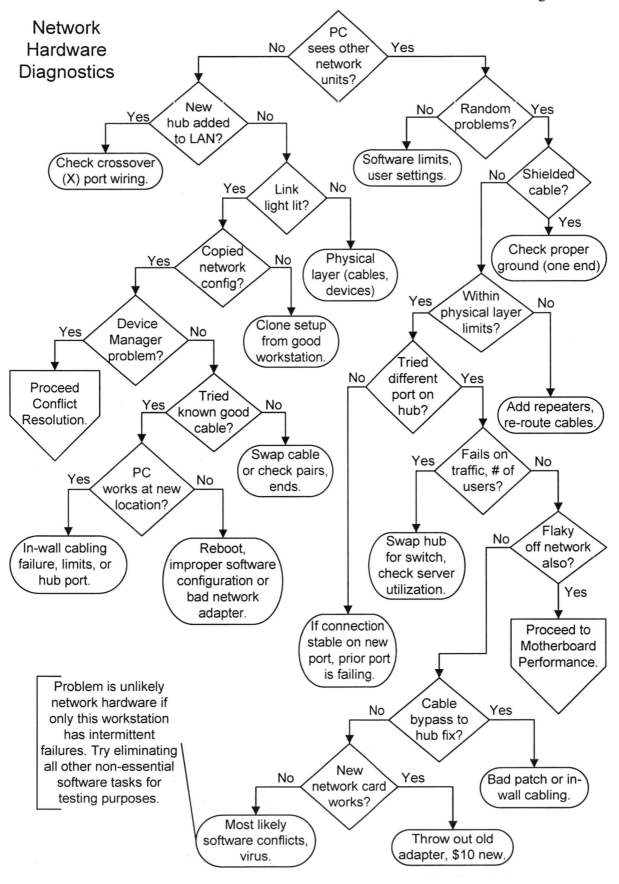

PC sees other network units?

- No → **New hub added to LAN?**
  - Yes → Check crossover (X) port wiring.
  - No → **Link light lit?**
    - Yes → **Copied network config?**
      - Yes → **Device Manager problem?**
        - Yes → Proceed Conflict Resolution.
        - No → **Tried known good cable?**
          - Yes → **PC works at new location?**
            - Yes → In-wall cabling failure, limits, or hub port.
            - No → Reboot, improper software configuration or bad network adapter.
          - No → Swap cable or check pairs, ends.
      - No → Clone setup from good workstation.
    - No → Physical layer (cables, devices)
- Yes → **Random problems?**
  - No → Software limits, user settings.
  - Yes → **Shielded cable?**
    - No → **Within physical layer limits?**
      - Yes → **Tried different port on hub?**
        - No → If connection stable on new port, prior port is failing.
        - Yes → **Fails on traffic, # of users?**
          - Yes → Swap hub for switch, check server utilization.
          - No → **Flaky off network also?**
            - No → **Cable bypass to hub fix?**
              - No → **New network card works?**
                - No → Most likely software conflicts, virus.
                - Yes → Throw out old adapter, $10 new.
              - Yes → Bad patch or in-wall cabling.
            - Yes → Proceed to Motherboard Performance.
      - No → Add repeaters, re-route cables.
    - Yes → Check proper ground (one end)

Problem is unlikely network hardware if only this workstation has intermittent failures. Try eliminating all other non-essential software tasks for testing purposes.

Network Hardware Diagnostics

Does the PC (Workstation) see any network resources, servers, other workstations? Note that some versions of networking software display "remembered" resources, even when the PC can't access them, so you'll need to actually click on a given resource to see if it's really available.

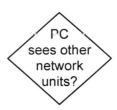

Have you recently added a network hub? Is the workstation the first workstation on a new hub, being stacked or chained to existing hub(s)? When connecting hubs or switches with twisted pair (RJ-45 connector) cabling, whether 10BaseT , 100BaseT or Gigabyte (1000BaseT), make sure that you either connect to an "X" port (uplink port), or use a special crossover cable. A crossover cable, unlike a straight through cable, connects pins 1 and 2 on one end to 3 and 6 on the other end and vice versa for 10BaseT and 100BaseT, and also connects pins 4 and 5 with 7 and 8 on the other end and vice versa for 1000BaseT. When building crossover cables, you must use a twisted pair for each named pair for noise protection. If you do have an X or uplink port, you normally see that it is connected to an adjacent port by a line or other symbol. You can only use one or the other, since they are using the same physical circuitry, with the X port making the pair reversal. Hubs have a power transformer that needs to be plugged into a live outlet.

Most network adapters have one or more onboard LEDs right next to the RJ-45 port to show the status of the link and network activity (traffic). Green is good for a link, a blinking LED next to it indicates traffic, or if they conserved on LEDs, the link LED will blink. No link light indicates there's a break in your physical layer. Check the physical connectors at all points on your network in the failed path, and make sure that you are within all of the limits for your physical layer in terms of number of workstations and distances. Swap the laptop's networking cable to another port on the router or hub and see if it works.

Have you cloned the software configuration from another workstation on the network (everything but the unique portion of the IP address, assuming you're set up for TCP/IP)? It's too easy to make a mistake with which protocol should be the default or with the spelling of a Workgroup, etc. At an active workstation, go through every option in the network setup and print screen every page and sub page that comes up. Keep it around for future reference when you run into networking problems with a similar workstation. If this is the first workstation on the network, or the second on a peer-to-peer, go with the defaults and make use of the operating system's built in troubleshooter, at least in Windows versions. Your problem is most likely software

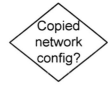

configuration, which is far too in depth to address in the chart. When in doubt, reboot.

Does the Device Manager see the network adapter and report no conflicts? Try reinstalling the driver and rebooting. In Windows, start by deleting the existing network device in Device Manager. If Windows still won't recognize the network adapter, it could be a conflict with another hardware adapter or it could be faulty. If the adapter is built-in, either on the motherboard or in a notebook, try restoring the defaults in CMOS Setup. Proceed to the Conflict Resolution flowchart.

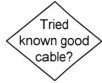

Tried known good cable? Even if the link light is lit, it doesn't mean your cable is capable of carrying network traffic. An incredible number of techs make these cables wrong out of sheer laziness or ignorance. Don't say, "But it's a new cable!" Four conductors are actually used for normal implementations 10BaseT and 100BaseT, and the wiring is straight through, 1-1, 2-2, 3-3, 6-6. Pins 1 and 2 and pins 3 and 6 must each use a twisted pair, or the longer runs will fail and shorter runs will act unpredictably. Gigabit, or 1000BaseT cables, use all 4 pairs, with 4-4, 5-5 adding one pair and 7-7, 8-8 adding the other. In addition, visually inspect connectors to make sure they are solid and wired properly (shared pairs listed above). Squint into the transparent connector and try to take note of the color coding for each pin. Then go look at the other end of the cable and make sure that the color coding is the same, AND that a pair (i.e, blue, blue stripe) is used for the pair 1 and 2, 3 and 6, etc.

Take the PC (just the system box which some people call the CPU) to another workstation location and swap it out with that PC. If you get right on the network, that tells you that the physical link to the location where it failed is bad. That could be the patch cable, the in-wall wiring, or the port on the hub it connects to. If it doesn't work at the new location, that tells you it's either the network adapter or the software configuration. If it's an add-in adapter and you have a spare, by all means try swapping it out, but the software settings are more often the culprit. Make sure the driver is up-to-date and the correct version for the OS, make sure that you have cloned all the settings (except the machine name or final IP address) from a working machine, and try going through the OS troubleshooting steps.

Are your network access problems of a random or intermittent nature? Check for loose connectors. It's very easy to install a RJ-45 connector improperly or fail to crimp it tightly enough to hold to the cable such that it loosens up with just a minor physical movement. The problem might also be interference somewhere in the cable run. Make sure it's not draped over the back of a CRT or running directly over florescent lights or other noisy RF emitters. You could be experiencing software conflicts with other processes on the PC. You can try eliminating all tasks except the minimal network configuration and do some large file movements to see if the hardware layer is solid. More likely it's simply the loading of the network, a traffic jam, or you're exceeding the number of simultaneous users supported by the hardware (including wireless) or the software.

Are you using Shielded Twisted Pair (STP) or any other cable type with a non-signaling shield? Note that this is not the usual case for twisted pair cabling. Make sure that the shield is grounded at one end only, or you could end up with a ground loop and a constant leakage current. If it's not grounded at either end, it may act as an antenna to pick up and disperse interference. Also, make sure that your cables, even when grounded, are intelligently routed. Stay away from transformers, high current junctions, heavy equipment that can induce lots of electrical noise, though it's primarily the higher frequencies you need to worry about.

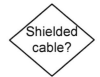

Are you within the physical layer limits for your network? This applies to both wired and wireless networks. Don't go by the number in the IEEE standard, use the limit in the hub, switch or base station documentation. Be aware that the distance limitations are based on a normal operating environment with the proper cabling or antennas installed. If your cables are made wrong, routed poorly, or are low quality, the limits will be reduced. Rerouting cables, adding repeaters (amplifiers) or eliminating sources of interference can increase the reach of your network.

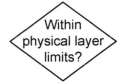

Have you tried a different port on the hub? There's no rule that says hubs have to fail all at once, and even though a performance degradation of a single port is a rarity, it's worth trying. It could also be that the cable end plugged into the hub wasn't crimped on as tightly as it could have been, causing the performance of the link to be dependent on the exact position of the cable, an unacceptable situation.

Does the problem, be it lost connections, slow performance or anything else, occur during periods when network traffic is high or a large number of users are logged on? There are many reasons a network can bog down or have trouble in high traffic or high user count situations, including the natural limitations of the technologies being used. In general, if you are using a passive hub, you can greatly increase your network performance during high traffic periods by swapping the hub for an active switch. Also, if you are running a hybrid LAN, with a mix of 10BaseT and 100BaseT and 1000BaseT adapters, you should think about upgrading them all to 1000BaseT, providing the cable plant is all Cat 5, which it better be!

Is the PC flaky when it's not on the network? If so, don't waste any more time on network diagnostics, proceed to Motherboard, CPU and RAM failure and look for the symptoms the PC is displaying. This isn't a good test of software problems, since you run different applications and have different resource usage when you're connected to the network.

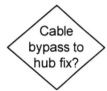

You should always have a proven long bypass cable for testing, that you can run directly from the workstation to the hub without going through walls, ceilings, etc. Make sure you are within the distance limits for twisted pair, wireless and IR, and within the total number of active stations limit for wireless and IR. Check for physical cable damage. The sheathing on the Cat 5 cables is thin and the inner conductors can be easily broken if the cable is stretched or crimped.

Does a new network adapter fix the problem? New PCI network adapters cost less than $10, so there's no reason not to try one. If you're running a wireless network with notebooks and add on wireless adapters, borrow one from a good unit. If the new network adapter hasn't fixed the problem and you've gone through all the physical layer diagnostics to get here, it's a software issue.

Peripheral Failure

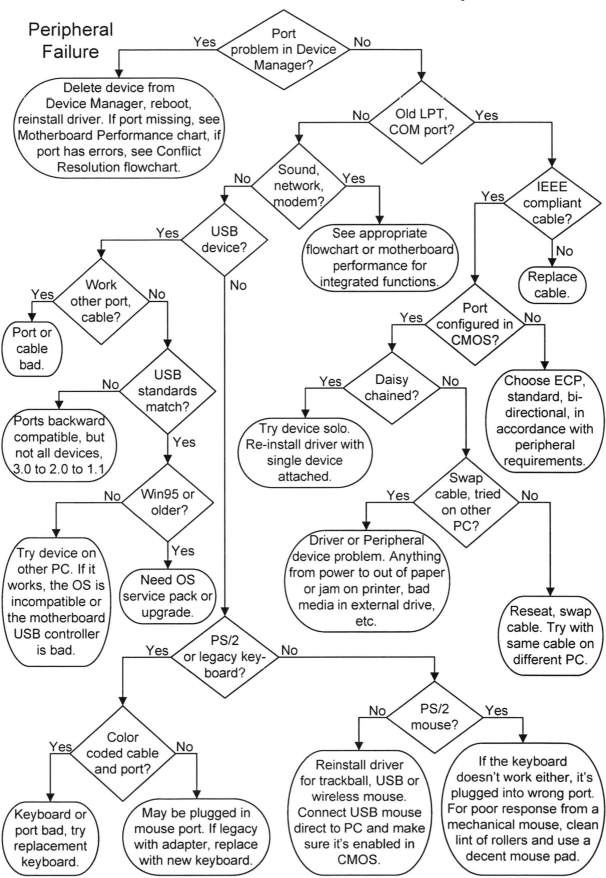

Port problem in Device Manager?

Yes → Delete device from Device Manager, reboot, reinstall driver. If port missing, see Motherboard Performance chart, if port has errors, see Conflict Resolution flowchart.

No → **Old LPT, COM port?**

No → **Sound, network, modem?**

Yes → See appropriate flowchart or motherboard performance for integrated functions.

No → **USB device?**

Yes → **Work other port, cable?**

Yes → Port or cable bad.

No → **USB standards match?**

No → Ports backward compatible, but not all devices, 3.0 to 2.0 to 1.1

Yes → **Win95 or older?**

No → Try device on other PC. If it works, the OS is incompatible or the motherboard USB controller is bad.

Yes → Need OS service pack or upgrade.

USB device? No → **PS/2 or legacy keyboard?**

Yes → **Color coded cable and port?**

Yes → Keyboard or port bad, try replacement keyboard.

No → May be plugged in mouse port. If legacy with adapter, replace with new keyboard.

No → **PS/2 mouse?**

No → Reinstall driver for trackball, USB or wireless mouse. Connect USB mouse direct to PC and make sure it's enabled in CMOS.

Yes → If the keyboard doesn't work either, it's plugged into wrong port. For poor response from a mechanical mouse, clean lint of rollers and use a decent mouse pad.

Old LPT, COM port? Yes → **IEEE compliant cable?**

Yes → **Port configured in CMOS?**

No → Replace cable.

Port configured in CMOS? Yes → **Daisy chained?**

Yes → Try device solo. Re-install driver with single device attached.

No → **Swap cable, tried on other PC?**

Yes → Driver or Peripheral device problem. Anything from power to out of paper or jam on printer, bad media in external drive, etc.

No → Reseat, swap cable. Try with same cable on different PC.

Port configured in CMOS? No → Choose ECP, standard, bi-directional, in accordance with peripheral requirements.

Peripheral Failure

Is the port to which your peripheral is hooked up present and healthy in Device Manager? You can access Device Manager a half dozen different ways in most Windows operating systems, but the most straightforward (no right clicking, etc.) is to go through Control Panel > System. If there are any notations next to the ports in Device Manager, such as "!" or "?", there's a conflict or a problem with the driver. Try deleting the device from Device Manager, rebooting, and letting Windows find and reinstall it. If it's not a standard device, you'll need the driver from the manufacturer. Since all of the I/O ports in modern PCs are integrated on the motherboard, that means re-installing the motherboard driver.

Is the peripheral connected to an old parallel port (LPT) or serial communications (COM) port? The LPT port would be a 25 pin female port on the back of your PC, COM ports can be 9 pin female or 25 pin male. Newer motherboards have completely dispensed with these old style ports in favor of USB, you're unlikely to see them on a PC built in the last ten years. There are a few devices other than old printers that may use the parallel port, primarily older scanners, but also some external drives. Once the most common methods for connecting peripherals to PCs, COM ports have been rendered obsolete by the addition of a dedicated PS/2 mouse port and USB ports for connecting most other devices. Dumb terminals and old digital cameras came with a serial port option, and early dial-up modems used serial ports.

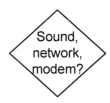

If you're having problems with speakers, microphones, headsets, with your network or modem, these may be termed peripherals but we deal with them on their own flowcharts in this book. The ports and controllers for the sound, network and dial-up modem will usually be integrated on the motherboard in recent PC's, so you should refer to the motherboard performance flowchart as well.

Is the peripheral a USB device? USB is the primary way modern peripherals are attached to PCs, and it's also the most idiot proof. The cables for standard devices can only be plugged in one way and the ends aren't reversible. The flat rectangular end of the cable plugs into the PC and the square end plugs into the device. If you have more USB devices than ports, you can add an external USB hub to provide more ports. However, some USB devices (those without their own power supply) are actually powered by the PC through the USB port and may not work if they are connected through a hub port that doesn't meet that power demand. If you are having a problem with a device connected through a hub, try connecting it directly to the USB port on the PC.

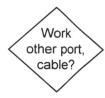

The first step when you're having trouble with any USB peripheral is to try it on a different USB port, and then swap the USB cable if it still doesn't work. USB ports mounted on the motherboard can fail mechanically or electrically, and it's not unusual to break a port clean off the motherboard or have the plastic insulator fall out after tripping over the cord. If any of the USB ports show a problem in Device Manager, deleting them and letting Windows reinstall them on the next boot may help.

Do the USB standards match? The most recent version of USB is 3.0, while most PCs (unless they are brand-new) sport USB 2.0 or even USB 1.1 ports. While a USB 3.0 or 2.0 port should support older devices, a new USB peripheral may not work on an older USB port due to speed or power considerations. For Blu Ray or DVD recorders, the speed is a real issue since buffer underruns will ruin the disc you're recording. For hard drives and many other devices, as long as the USB port supplies sufficient power, they'll usually just run at a slower data speed.

If you aren't running an antique with Windows 95, the last test is to install the peripheral on a different computer and see if it works there. If it does, you know that the problem is either due to the software installed (the application or the driver, which may be incompatible with your OS version) or port failure. You can confirm port failure by borrowing some other known good USB device, like a memory stick, and seeing if that works on any of your USB ports. If not, as long as you have an open expansion slot in the PC, you can buy a PCI adapter with the latest USB technology.

The original version of Windows 95, release 1 or version A, doesn't support USB. Fastest way to figure out your Widows 95 version is to right-click on My Computer and pick System Properties. Even if you have physical USB ports on the motherboard or on an add-in adapter, you need to upgrade your Windows version to support USB. Windows 95 versions B and C do support USB, though you may have to manually install a few files to get it to work, and '95 is no longer supported by Microsoft. The instructions for adding USB support to versions B and C of Windows 95 are too long to include here, but can be easily found by doing a Google search with the keywords: "Windows 95 USB upgrade."

Is the problem with a keyboard, either PS/2 or legacy? Keyboards aren't worth fooling around with, as new ones are dirt cheap and last longer than old expensive keyboards in any case. Keyboards can cause apparently unrelated fatal errors. I've seen an old keyboard with a PS/2 adapter cause Windows 2000 to do the "Blue screen of death" on boot.

Took forever to troubleshoot, who checks keyboards? If you spill coffee all over your keyboard and it doesn't cause an immediate failure, you can disconnect it from the PC and try rinsing it out with warm water. Don't try hooking it up to the PC again until you're sure it's had ample time to dry out, at least over night. If you're using a USB keyboard for the first time, make sure USB keyboard is enabled in CMOS Setup.

Is your problem with a PS/2 port mouse? If the keyboard doesn't work either, you probably got the ports reversed. Skip down two paragraphs to the "Color coded cables?" diamond. Mechanical mouse performance degrades over time as the rollers pick up lint. A mechanical mouse can be cleaned by popping the retaining plate off the bottom, dropping the ball out in your hand, and picking the lint off the rollers. A mouse pad will improve your mouse performance, but not the shiny plastic kind that advertise something and actually cause traction problems.

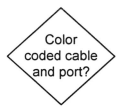

PS/2 mouse?

Problems with an optical USB mouse, wireless mouse or trackball are usually due a device driver that's not up-to-date for the operating system. Go to the web site of the device manufacturer and download the latest driver for your operating system. Try running USB mice directly from the PC if you are plugged into a hub. If you're having intermittent problems with a wireless mouse, it may be interference, particularly if it occurs while you are using a wireless phone. The only way to tell if a mouse is bad is to install it on a known good PC, along with the proper drivers if it's a "super" mouse.

Cleaning a mechanical mouse:

www.fonerbooks.com /r_mouse.htm

Are the mouse and keyboard ports color coded? The PS/2 connectors used on all new mice and keyboards can be accidentally plugged into the wrong port, which is particularly easy to do if you're working under a desk. If you mix up the mouse and the keyboard, Windows will usually complain that no mouse is present when it loads. Keyboard connectors are coded purple, mouse connectors are coded green. If the ports aren't color coded, there should be little mouse and keyboard symbols pointing out which is which. If you have the connector fully seated in the correct port and the keyboard or mouse is undetected or doesn't work, replace it.

Color coded cable and port?

Are you using an IEEE compliant cable? If you tried saving a few bucks by using a "found in the basement" printer cable and you're having problems, it's the first thing to check. If the connectors on your printer cable aren't molded (i.e, if they are hollow pieces of plastic snapped or screwed together), it's a safe bet the cable isn't compliant.

IEEE compliant cable?

Have you checked the port configuration in CMOS Setup? Depending on the age of your BIOS, you may have the option to select the standard (old fashioned) mode, bi-directional or ECP. The documentation with your printer or parallel port peripheral will tell you whether or not you need to set a specific mode in CMOS Setup. If your ports are not integrated on the motherboard, they are most likely included on an old SIDE (Super IDE) controller, but the settings for these are set by jumpers on the card, and unless the settings are silk screened next to the jumpers, you'll never find them. You might be able to find an early PCI card that supports serial ports for old terminals if your ports have failed and you are absolutely desperate.

Is your parallel port device daisy chained? This was pretty popular with scanners before USB took over, and it was often problematic. The order you installed the devices and the drivers could make a difference, and some printers and scanners wouldn't work on the same port no matter what you did. The best test is to uninstall the drivers for any parallel port peripherals installed, reboot, then try installing the problem device as stand-alone on the port.

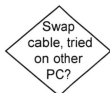

Have you tried swapping the cable? Even if it's a brand new, 100% guaranteed and IEEE compliant, it could be bad out of the box. Cables pass much of their lives behind desks and on floors, so it's also quite possible that the cable has been damaged. Make sure you do all the idiot checks, like that the peripheral's external power plugged in to a good outlet. In the end, the best way to test whether or not a peripheral has failed or if it's a port or software problem is to try installing it on another PC.

Laser printer not ready errors are commonly paper related - too much, too little or jam. Too much paper in your laser printer input tray can cause continual input jams, or even a "No Paper" error. Not enough paper can also cause a "No Paper" error, particularly on top fed lasers. Paper jams that won't go away or repeat after you clear the old paper are often due to teeny bits of paper torn off and jammed in the paper travel path. Using paper that's too flimsy or too damp can increase these problems.

Inkjet printer paper problems are usually caused by too much paper in the hopper. Other problems are ink cartridges not fully seated, forgetting to remove the protective tape from a new cartridge, and the usual cable and port issues. Out of warrantee inkjet repair isn't even worth thinking about unless you paid several hundred dollars for a business version. Replacement printers with rebates are often cheaper than cartridges.

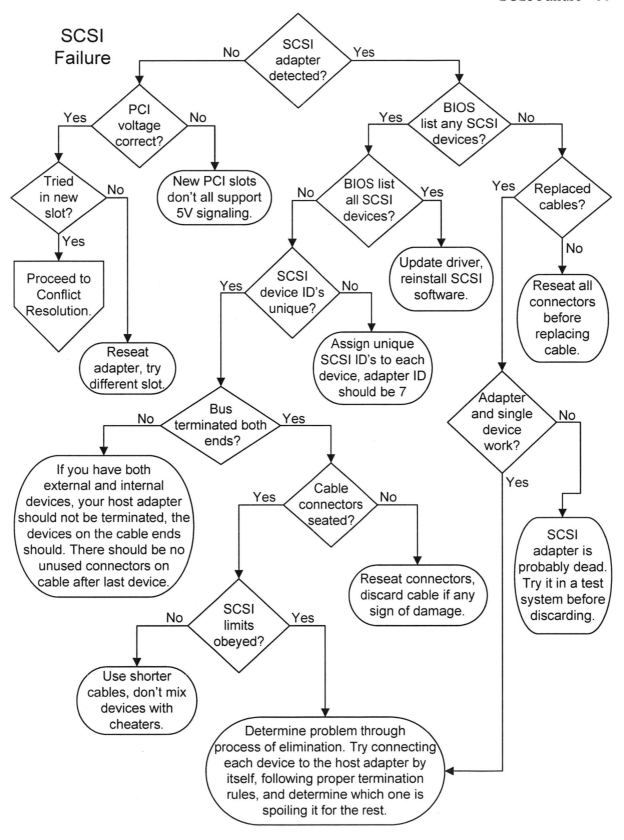

SCSI Failure

SCSI Failure

Is your SCSI adapter recognized by the BIOS at power up? All modern SCSI adapters carry their own SCSI BIOS that must be recognized and loaded by the PC BIOS at boot time. There are some ancient "dumb" SCSI cards kicking around for running scanners or old CD drives which are run through an operating system driver, but I've never seen a PCI version. When the SCSI adapter BIOS loads, it will flash an on-screen message, like "Press CRTL-A" to access SCSI BIOS (Adaptec).

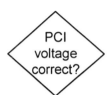

SCSI adapters are pretty sophisticated, practically single board computers. There are lots of 5V PCI SCSI adapters still kicking around, even though many new PCI slots only support 3.3V adapters. This is the first thing to check in the documentation of your SCSI adapter and motherboard.

Have you tried moving the adapter to a new slot? Make sure you screw in the hold-down and that the card is evenly seated in the slot. The sophistication of SCSI adapters makes them a little more finicky than other PCI adapters, and the order in which the PC BIOS reckons them up may make a difference. You can go into CMOS Setup and play with the PCI or PCI Express bus settings if the adapter BIOS won't load. Some SCSI adapters are even equipped with an onboard LED to confirm the adapter status and report error codes. If you can't get the adapter to report in on power up, proceed to Conflict Resolution.

Does the BIOS screen generated by the SCSI Adapter list any of the SCSI devices you have installed? If the SCSI support is integrated on the motherboard, this information may be combined with the standard BIOS boot screen. The device should be identified by manufacturer, model, SCSI ID and LUN (Logical Unit Number, largely irrelevant unless you're building a juke box). The SCSI adapter itself should appear in this accounting, generally on SCSI ID 7.

Does the SCSI BIOS see all of the SCSI devices you've installed? If it does, whatever access problem you're having is most likely the result of outdated operating system drivers or SCSI application software. If everything works fine but you have intermittent SCSI problems, proceed as if you had answered "no" to this question, and pay special attention to termination, cable quality and SCSI limit issues.

Are all of your SCSI device IDs unique? It's almost certain that you believe they are unique, since you set them before you installed the SCSI devices, but double check. The most common failing that can leave you with two devices sharing the same SCSI ID is a misplaced

or defective jumper. It's not the black plastic that makes the connection, it's the little metal spring clip within the plastic housing. If the jumper is defective, it won't set the ID bit. Some SCSI jumpers are so tiny that it's easy to miss one of the pins when you place them. If you were trying to set two drives on SCSI addresses -"0" and "2," and the jumper on the ID 1 pair missed one of the posts, you'd end up with two drives set to ID 0.

Although the binary addressing should be fully explicated in your SCSI documentation, you may be working with second hand stuff, so the general deal is as follows:

Older, "Narrow" SCSI controllers supported up to 8 devices (including the controller), so they required three ID bits to select a unique set of addresses. The standard is to label these as, ID 0, ID 1, and ID 2, where ID 0 is the low bit. An "X" represents a jumper.

Addr	ID 2	ID 1	ID 0
0	0	0	0
1	0	0	X
2	0	X	0
3	0	X	X
4	X	0	0
5	X	0	X
6	X	X	0
7	X	X	X

Newer, "Wide", SCSI controllers and devices support up to 16 addresses, where the controller takes up one, so a single controller can support 15 devices. The only difference between the jumper setting for new and old devices is that newer devices have a fourth SCSI ID selection, ID 3, which is jumpered for addresses 8 - 15. The lower ID bits are set exactly as above, but you add 8 to each address when ID 3 is jumpered.

Is the SCSI bus terminated on both ends? This has gotten particularly tricky since some new SCSI adapters can auto sense termination requirements and handle it themselves, and the newer LVD scheme provides termination on one end of the cable. The new SCSI devices that work with the Wide LVD cable should ship with termination disabled, though they may have onboard termination available for compatibility with the older SCSI technology. You really need to check the documentation or hop onto the manufacturer's website for details about the SCSI termination for particular devices.

The important thing to know about SCSI termination is that both ends of the bus must be terminated. The bus is a physical thing, not a theoretical conception. All of the devices on a SCSI bus share the same parallel transmission line for data and signals, and the devices at both ends of the line (or the line itself) must provide termination. There are four basic possibilities for a SCSI bus architecture.

1) You have an internal SCSI adapter and one or more internal SCSI devices. The devices are attached to the SCSI adapter by a ribbon cable. The SCSI adapter is at one end of the bus and must have termination enabled or set on automatic (usually done through the SCSI BIOS, as opposed to a physical jumper). The SCSI device at the end of the bus must be terminated if you're using a 50 wire ribbon cable, or it must be attached to the last connector before the terminator on the end of a 68 wire LVD cable.

2) You have an internal SCSI adapter and one or more external SCSI devices. The SCSI adapter must be terminated, and the last external SCSI device on the daisy chain must be terminated. Some external SCSI devices are equipped with a termination switch, others require installation of a SCSI terminator on their outgoing SCSI connector.

3) You have one or more internal SCSI devices and one or more external SCSI devices, all attached to the same internal SCSI adapter. The last external device on the daisy chain must be terminated and the last internal device on a 50 pin ribbon cable must be terminated or attached to the last connector on the 68 wire LVD cable. The adapter must have termination disabled because it is in the middle of the bus.

4) You combine any of the above scenarios with a SCSI adapter that supports two internal SCSI busses, a high speed 68 wire LVD bus and an older 50 pin bus. If you have both types of SCSI devices, it's recommended that you install them on separate cables for best performance, even though adapters or dual connectors may be available for the device. Any time you have two internal cables attached to the SCSI adapter, they must be terminated according to their type. The last connector on the 50 wire cable must be connected to a terminated drive, while the last connector on the 68 wire LVD cable must be connected to an unterminated drive.

Are all of the cable connectors seated? When you start getting up to 50 pins mating into a connector, it can take a bit of pushing. After you think the connector is seated, push on each end of the connector in turn to make sure that it isn't rocking on an obstruction in the middle. A properly seated cable connector won't move, wherever you push on it. The newer 68 pin LVD connectors do it in a smaller form than the

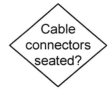

older 50 pin connectors, and the unfortunate side-effect is that the pins themselves are more fragile. Be careful when seating the connectors, and if you have to pull the connector off for troubleshooting, inspect the pins to make sure none are bent over.

Have you obeyed all the SCSI limits? These limits are entirely dependent on the SCSI adapter and devices you are using, not to mention the number of devices on the bus and the type and quality of the cables. Ultra SCSI 160, 320 and 640 have focused on data throughput rather than increasing the maximum bus length. The limitation subject is far too complicated for this discussion, but keep in mind it works both ways. For example, if you build your own cables, you can't put the connectors two inches apart just to keep the cabling in your case neat. There are minimum as well as maximum distances involved, depending on the SCSI technology and the speed at which you are running the bus.

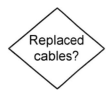

Have you replaced the cables? SCSI cables are the weak links in older machines, particularly when you've made and unmade the connectors a number of times. The stress relief on the connector can fail, particularly if you use the cable to pull the connection apart. Pushing the two halves back together just doesn't cut it in high speed communications.

Can you get the adapter to recognize a single device? If the adapter termination is on automatic, you can try putting it on manual and forcing termination on, though it's rarely the issue. If you're using an older Narrow SCSI device for the test, make sure it's terminated. If you're using a Wide device on an LVD cable, make sure it's unterminated and connected to the last connector on the terminated end of the LVD cable. If you can't get the SCSI adapter to see the device, try another one, if you have one available. Some SCSI adapters ship with pretty good onboard diagnostics, and there may be a further piece of diagnostic software available on the driver CD or the manufacturers web site. SCSI adapters are one of the higher quality items in the PC industry, but they do fail, so if you absolutely can't get a SCSI adapter to register a device, even when testing with multiple cables and devices, it may be dead.

If you get the SCSI adapter working with one or more devices but still have problems, it comes down to process of elimination. If it's a reliability issue, try running the bus at lower speed, or with the slower or older devices temporarily detached. If you never got all of the SCSI devices recognized, try them in different combinations and triple check the IDs, though it's always possible that some devices are good and others are dead.

Conflict
Resolution

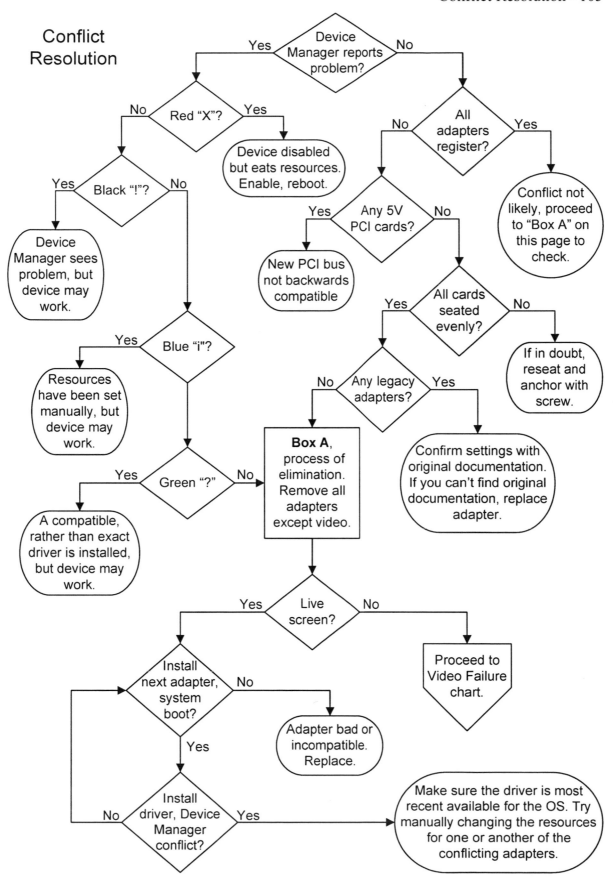

Conflict Resolution

Does Device Manager report a problem? When you view all of the installed devices by type in Device Manger, a problem is expressed by any extra symbol, like a "!" or a "?" appearing next to a device. If you see a problem, before you shut down and start ripping the machine apart, check if Device Manager can generate a conflict report. Double click on the problem device(s) or click on the little "+" to the left of any questionable devices to get the expanded view. When you double click on any specific piece of hardware in the expanded view and select the Resources tab, there's a little box in the lower half of the results that reports on conflicting devices. Write down any information in the box, rather than trusting it to memory.

Is there a red "X" next to the device that's not working? A red "X" means that the device has been disabled, but it still eats hardware resources and may cause conflicts with other installed devices. This information appears on the "General" tab of Device Manager, the first screen that comes up when you double click on a specific device. At the bottom of the screen there are two check boxes under the heading "Device Usage." If the "Disable in this hardware profile" box is checked, click in the box to uncheck it, then reboot.

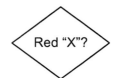

Is there a black "!" next to a device? Device Manager sees a problem, but the device may actually work. It could be that there's a conflict with another device, but the software driver is still capable of managing the input as long as you don't try using both conflicting devices at once. This was fairly common in the days before USB, when running out of Com ports was a common occurrence and sharing Com port IRQs was normal. Even if the device is working, you should check if there's a more recent driver available on the manufacturer's web site.

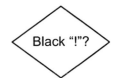

Is there a blue "i" next to a device? An "i" doesn't indicate a problem as much as a warning that the device's resources have been set manually. This could easily be the result of your having cleared up a conflict by manually forcing different resources on a device. If everything works fine, don't worry about it.

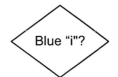

Is there a green "?" next to a device? The "?" means that a compatible device driver has been installed. If you're having any problem with a device, the driver is the first thing to check, and having a compatible driver, rather than an exact match from the manufacturer, is probably at fault. If you can't find the latest version on the web look through all your PC junk for the original driver disk. Unfortunately, I've encountered plenty of modems and the like for which the company had

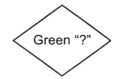

gone out of business and there was no way to find, much less determine, the exact driver for the device. If you have the patience to fool around with installing the generic operating system drivers for the device or downloading and trying close matches from the web, go ahead. If you're doing this for a business, replace the adapter; it's not worth the time.

Do all the adapters register? Is the BIOS or the operating system even aware that the adapter is installed? Even a legacy adapter should be found by whatever software driver or configuration application that it shipped with. If all the adapters are present and accounted for, and Device Manager didn't report any problems, the issue you're trying to diagnose probably isn't a conflict. However, if you've tried everything else, it's always possible, so skip to Box A and begin the process of elimination.

Do you have any 5V PCI cards? Depending on the age of your motherboard, it may be using one of the new PCI versions that are not backward compatible with the original 5V PCI cards. The fix for this is to replace the adapter, not the motherboard. The last pre-PCI Express specification, PCI 3.0, doesn't include support for 5V signaling, in response to the fact that many manufacturers had already dropped 5V signaling support from earlier PCI implementations.

Are all of the adapters seated evenly and secured? Actually, there are some alternative case designs that don't involve anchoring the adapter in place with a screw on the back rail. One approach is to lock all installed adapters in place with a single bar. However, it's not the top of the card but the contact edge you should be looking at. I've encountered plenty of adapters where the circuit board was improperly mounted on the metal bracket. Another possibility is short standoffs under the motherboard and a high rail on the case. If the contact edge of an adapter doesn't seat all the way into a slot and that adapter isn't being registered by the PC, you may have to straighten out the bend at the top bracket to let the card seat all the way.

Do you any legacy adapters installed? Legacy adapters, whether 8 or 16 bit ISA adapters, are very questionable in the current plug-n-play environment, even if the motherboard has an ISA slot to accept them. The card may feature physical jumpers or switches for allocating resources, or it may have shipped with a software configuration tool. If you don't have the original documentation, you can try going by the settings printed on the adapter, but I wouldn't waste too much time on it.

Box A. The brute force method to solving hardware conflicts is to begin by eliminating the conflict by eliminating all the optional adapters. Then you begin reinstalling the adapters, one at a time, until the conflict reappears. Not very high tech, but effective. Start by removing all of the add in adapters except the video card.

Do you get a live screen? The "live screen" referred to in this case is a boot screen generated by the BIOS or an operating system splash screen. It doesn't include any monitor generated messages like "No signal present." If you don't get a live screen, proceed to the Video Failure chart.

Does the system boot? Power down, unplug the system, and install the next adapter. When troubleshooting adapter conflicts, I tend to sequence them by cost, installing the most expensive adapter first. That way, when you do reach an adapter that's causing a conflict, you can try swapping it out with another rather than worrying which adapter is to blame. If installing an adapter actually prevents boot in an otherwise stable system, just replace the adapter.

Install the driver for the device you just installed. Does Device Manager now show a conflict? If not, power down and install the next adapter. If you do get a Device Manager conflict, make sure you have installed the latest possible version of the driver for your operating system by checking the manufacturer's web site. If you are using the latest version of the driver, manually change the setting of the adapter you just installed. If Device Manager won't let you change the individual resource settings, try selecting a different standard configuration, if available. Make sure you have the BIOS defaults set in CMOS Setup.

If that still doesn't do it, return to Box A, strip out all of the adapters except the video and reboot so Windows can reset the registry. Next, start the process again, but this time install the problem adapter first, and find out if the conflict is with the video card or motherboard. If so, replace it. If not, continue with the process, and the operating system may clear the conflict just based on the order the drivers are installed.

Your First Sale

Book Excerpt from "Start Your Own Computer Business"

You've sold your first PC to your mother's friend Doris, and then find out that whether you order it assembled or in pieces, there's not going to be any profit because you included Windows in the price but forgot to add in the cost. This drives you to ignore the top two tiers of distribution and go straight to the small importers with the aggressive pricing. You know the stuff is good because it says so on the fax. By using PriceWatch.com and going with the most aggressive pricing for each part, you figure you can scrape out a fifty dollar profit. You order an ATX case, keyboard and mouse from one place; a motherboard, CPU, RAM, hard drive and OEM Windows from a second place; and a floppy drive, video adapter, CD-ROM, modem, monitor and soundcard from a third place. Even the guy on the other coast promises you'll have the stuff within a week.

The next day, the ATX case and power supply show up with the keyboard and mouse, and the UPS gal wants a check for $80. "What's this?" you say. "The parts cost was $71." The UPS gal explains that the shipping cost was $5 and the COD tag allowing you to pay with company check cost $4. You pay and go back to your spreadsheet to see where this is heading. Three days later, the motherboard, CPU, hard drive and Windows show up from the middle of the country by Fed-X. You feel pretty good until you look at the invoice, which shows your credit card was billed for $355. Wait a minute, the parts total was $321. The bottom of the invoice shows a $29 item for 2nd day shipping, and another $5 for handling and insurance. You call the supplier, who reminds you that you wanted it by Thursday, and that he did tell you he was waiting for a shipment of RAM to arrive Tuesday morning. Well, at least you can give yourself credit that you bought the motherboard, CPU and RAM from a single vendor. Doing otherwise before your really know your vendors is pretty risky.

After assembling the parts that have arrived, you settle in to wait for the package from the other coast. It shows up after a week with a COD tag for exactly what you thought you were paying! Great! You pay, unpack the stuff to finish building your first PC and find the modem is missing. You read the invoice and see that the modem was "backordered" and the COD amount didn't include it. You run to the phone and call the vendor, who tells you, "Don't worry, it went out three days ago." "Call me next time before you backorder something on me," you yell at the voice. After you hang up, the voice says "Jerk." Three days later, the $29 modem shows up with a COD tag for $38.

Hey, he did have to handle it separately, and the $4 for the COD is a constant. It's not the modem you ordered, but at this point, Doris is calling every day (she pre-paid), so you swallow a total of $81 ($9 + $34 + $29 +$9) in shipping, handling and insurance costs. You begin to see where ordering everything from one nearby vendor, preferably with net terms (non-COD) or a credit card, makes more sense than parting the thing out all over creation.

You put all the paperwork in a file folder labeled "Doris" and file it. This is really a critical step. Nobody will take defective stuff back without paperwork, unless you have a real good relationship and can get the salesman to look it up on their computer system for you. You finish putting the PC together, load Windows, and everything is great. You load all the driver CDs for the video, modem, and sound card (you forgot to include speakers in the price), and Windows now takes twice as long to boot. Par for the course. The monitor gives off an odor like burning plastic on an ocean breeze, but you figure that will clear up. You run ScanDisk a couple times, wonder what a 24 hour burn-in really means, and if you should spend a hundred dollars on some testing software. Unless you have money to burn, don't bother. Just leave the thing turned on overnight and check that it still works in the morning. It's a decent test, and you're doing a lot more than most guys I've known.

You put the PC in the car, and drive it to the customer's home. If you were a mail-order business you could leave it on the doorstep, ring the doorbell and run, but you aren't. You take the PC out of the box and plug everything together. Your customer turns it on, the Microsoft flag appears, so you leave your homemade business card and go home relieved that you only lost around $31 selling your first PC. You use a hobby knife to cut up the boxes that Doris didn't want and you put them out for recycling day. The foam peanuts you save, believing that eventually they'll come in handy- good luck. The next morning the phone rings, your first tech support call. Doris bought an inkjet printer at Staples (they had it cheaper than any price you could find) and it doesn't work - Staples tells her it sounds like a computer problem. You warn your mother's dearest and oldest friend that if it's not a computer problem, you'll have to charge her your $50 field service rate, and she agrees. You arrive at her house, and immediately see that she's trying to use old typewriter paper in the printer and the paper isn't heavy enough for the feeder, producing all sorts of jams and "printer not ready or not connected" errors. Since you only spend two minutes in the house and it's such a silly problem, you can't bring yourself to charge her.

Being the clever sort, you cut a deal with your local Internet Service Provider (ISP) where they promise to pay you $100 at the end of the year for each new customer you deliver to them. You call your customer, talk her out of going with AOL or Compuserve, which her son in Dallas has told her to get, and you drive out and create a dial-up-networking connection to her new ISP. You set her up with Internet Explorer and Outlook Express, spend two or three hours teaching her how to use e-mail and buy junk on E-Bay. Then you go home satisfied that you're now making the $35 to $50 an hour you always knew you were worth, even if you won't get it for twelve months.

Unfortunately, when her son visits for Christmas, he convinces her that she can save big bucks by signing a multi-year deal with a national provider, and your $100 miraculously vanishes. Adding insult to injury, the day after New Year's she calls you to say the modem isn't working anymore. On hearing that she has moved to AOL, you spend a half-hour on the phone angrily explaining that it's probably a software problem, and that you'll have to charge that elusive $50 field rate if you come out. She agrees, and you show up to find that the modem really did die.

You go home, pull out the "Doris" folder, call the vendor, who gives you an RMA (Return Merchandise Authorization) number and tells you he'll ship a replacement. You breathe a sigh of relief that the vendor is still in business, since you haven't talked to him in three months, and then send off the modem. After a week, you call, and he explains that he has to ship it back to his supplier, but they turn stuff around really fast, and you should have the replacement within two weeks. You give up and call your local importer and buy another $29 modem, paying with a credit card. It comes the next day and you install it. Doris is pretty upset at having been offline for a week, and suggests that maybe you've bitten off more than you can chew in "your little computer business." Two months later, her original modem arrives in a beat up package from some place you never heard of with a note saying they tested it fully and it worked for them. You put it in your own PC to test it and immediately smell smoke. Welcome to the PC business.

Excerpted from "Start Your Own Computer Business: Building a Successful PC Repair Business by Supporting Customers and Managing Money." by Morris Rosenthal, ISBN: 0-9723801-0-8

163 page paperback retails for $14.95, Ebook $11.95
Direct sales from - http://www.fonerbooks.com/border.htm

Breinigsville, PA USA
02 September 2009
223488BV00001B/5/P

9 780972 380171